Make Money with Price Action Trading

The Complete Guide to Succeeding in Financial Markets

Preface: Introduction to Trading Risks	**5**
1.1 What is Price Action Trading?	6
1.2 Historical Background and Evolution of Price Action Trading	7
1.3 Advantages and Disadvantages of Price Action Trading	8
Chapter 2: Price Chart Analysis	**10**
2.1 Using Japanese Candlesticks in Technical Analysis	10
2.2 Identifying Candlestick Patterns for Trading	11
2.3 Using Trendlines in Chart Analysis	14
2.4 Finding Support and Resistance Levels	16
Chapter 3: Trend Identification	**18**
3.1 Using Moving Averages to Identify Trends	18
3.2 Recognizing Trends with Highs and Lows Analysis	21
3.3 Trend Confirmation Using Supplementary Indicators	22
Chapter 4: Price Action-Based Trading Strategies	**25**
4.1 Trend Reversal Strategies	25
4.2 Trend Continuation Strategies	26
4.3 Trading Based on Fibonacci Retracements	28
4.4 Managing Entry and Exit Positions	30
Chapter 5: Risk and Money Management	**33**
5.1 Significance of Risk Management in Trading	33
5.2 Determining the Appropriate Position Size	34
5.3 Utilization of Stop-loss and Take-profit Orders	36
5.4 Techniques to Minimize Losses and Maximize Profits	37
Chapter 6: Trading Psychology	**41**
6.1 Emotional Control and Discipline in Trading	41
6.2: Stress and Anxiety Management in Trading	43
Chapter 7: Case Studies and Practical Examples	**48**
7.1 Analysis of Real Trades with Explained Entries and Exits	48
7.2 Reflections on the Decisions Made and the Results Obtained	51
Chapter 8: Advanced Price Action Trading Techniques	**52**
8.1 Utilizing Market Correlation to Enhance Trading Signals	52
8.2 Short-Term Trading vs. Long-Term Trading: Strategy Comparison	53
Chapter 9: Price Action Based Automated Trading	**56**
9.1 Introduction to Automated Trading Systems	56
9.2 Development of Algorithmic Trading Strategies	57
9.3: Backtesting and Optimization of Automated Strategies	58
9.4: Implementation and Monitoring of Automated Trading Systems	60
Chapter 10: Evolution and Adaptation in a Changing Market Environment	**62**
10.1 Importance of Adaptability in Trading	62
10.2 Continuous Review and Adjustment of Trading Strategies	63
10.3 Strategies for Dealing with Unexpected Events in the Markets	65
10.4 Long-Term Planning for Trading Sustainability	66
Chapter 11: Continuous Education and Resources for Traders	**69**

11.1 Importance of Ongoing Learning in Trading	69
11.2 Sources of Information and Education for Traders	70
11.3 Trading Communities and Support Networks for Traders	71
11.4 Investment in Professional Development Programs	72
Conclusion	**74**
Glossary	**75**
Frequently Asked Questions:	77
Personal Notes:	83

Preface: Introduction to Trading Risks

Before delving into the world of trading, it's essential to understand the inherent risks associated with this activity. Trading in financial markets offers profit opportunities, but it also comes with the risk of significant losses. It's important for every trader, whether novice or experienced, to recognize and proactively manage these risks.

One of the primary risks of trading is market volatility, which can lead to sudden and unpredictable price movements. These fluctuations can cause significant losses if positions are not managed properly. Additionally, financial markets can be influenced by economic, political, and geopolitical events, which can increase volatility and make trading riskier.

Another significant risk is market risk, which refers to the possibility that asset prices move unfavorably due to external factors beyond the trader's control. Fluctuations in exchange rates, interest rates, and commodity prices can all affect trading performance.

Furthermore, trading involves specific risks related to the use of leverage, which allows traders to control larger positions with a smaller initial capital. While leverage can increase potential profits, it also amplifies potential losses, making risk management all the more crucial.

Finally, it's important to recognize the risk of total capital loss. Even with careful risk management and thorough analysis, there's always the possibility of significant losses, particularly due to unexpected market movements or irrational market behavior.

In conclusion, trading carries significant risks that must be considered by every trader. It's essential to understand these risks and adopt appropriate risk management strategies to protect capital and maximize chances of success in financial markets.

Chapter 1: Foundations of Price Action Trading

1.1 What is Price Action Trading?

Price action trading is a trading method that focuses on directly analyzing price movements on trading charts to make buying or selling decisions. Unlike other approaches that rely on complex technical indicators, this method relies on price patterns and interpreting market movements without depending on external indicators.

This approach is based on the idea that all the information needed to make trading decisions is already reflected in the price movements themselves. Prices move predictably in recurring patterns, allowing traders to anticipate future market movements.

Analyzing price charts is at the core of price action trading. Traders study Japanese candlesticks, trendlines, support and resistance levels, and other chart elements to identify market patterns and trends. For example, a bullish trend reversal may be signaled by a series of bearish candlesticks followed by a bullish reversal candlestick pattern, called a morning star, at a key support level.

Once a trader identifies a pattern or trend on the chart, they can make trading decisions accordingly. For example, if they identify a bullish trend with a series of higher highs and higher lows, they may look to buy when the price bounces off a key support level. Similarly, if they identify a bearish trend with a series of lower lows and lower highs, they may look to sell when the price reaches a key resistance level.

Price action trading offers several advantages over other trading approaches. Firstly, it simplifies the analysis process by focusing on a single source of information, namely price movements. This allows traders to reduce confusion and make clearer and faster decisions. Additionally, this approach is often considered more objective because it is based on real market data rather than subjective interpretations of technical indicators.

Furthermore, price action trading can be applied to any financial market, from stocks and currencies to commodities and cryptocurrencies. This makes it a versatile method that can be adapted to different trading styles and timeframes.

However, despite its many advantages, price action trading is not without its limitations. Firstly, it requires a solid understanding of technical analysis and regular practice to develop the skills necessary for effective application. Additionally, some traders may find it challenging to stick to such a simplistic approach, especially if they are accustomed to using a variety of technical indicators in their analysis.

Finally, like any trading strategy, price action trading carries risks, and it is essential for traders to implement appropriate risk management techniques to protect their capital.

In summary, price action trading is a trading method that focuses on directly analyzing price movements on trading charts to identify potential trading opportunities. This approach relies on a deep understanding of market psychology and price patterns, and it can be successfully applied to different financial markets with the appropriate practice and experience.

1.2 Historical Background and Evolution of Price Action Trading

Price action trading has a rich and complex history that traces back to the earliest forms of commerce and speculation. As we delve into its history, we can observe how this trading method has evolved and adapted to economic, technological, and social changes throughout the ages.

Ancient Origins

The origins of price action trading can be traced back to the emergence of commodity markets and trade fairs in ancient societies. In these environments, merchants traded goods such as grain, livestock, and textiles based on supply and demand, with prices often determined through public auctions or direct negotiations. These early markets were driven by price fluctuations, and merchants developed skills to interpret price movements and identify profit opportunities. This direct observation of prices and market trends laid the foundation for price action trading, even in an era where modern technical analysis tools did not exist.

Evolution Over Time

Over the centuries, price action trading has continued to evolve with the advent of capitalism, stock exchanges, and more sophisticated financial instruments. As financial markets developed, traders and investors devised new analysis techniques to assess prices of stocks, bonds, and other financial assets. A key milestone in the evolution of price action trading was the introduction of Japanese candlestick charts to the Western world. Originating in Japan in the 18th century, these charts were popularized in the 1980s by American trader Steve Nison. Japanese candlesticks provided a visual representation of price movements, highlighting open, close, high, and low levels for each time period. This approach made it easier for traders to identify patterns and trends on charts, laying the groundwork for modern technical analysis.

Contemporary Popularity

Today, price action trading is widely practiced by traders worldwide and has become a dominant approach in the trading field. Technological advancements have facilitated access to real-time market data, enabling traders to analyze price movements with increased precision and efficiency. Furthermore, the evolution of trading platforms has allowed traders to apply price action-based strategies to a variety of financial markets, including stocks, currencies, futures, and cryptocurrencies. This versatility has contributed to the growing popularity of price action trading among traders of all experience levels.

In conclusion, price action trading has a long and fascinating history that reflects human ingenuity and adaptability in the realms of commerce and investment. From its humble beginnings in ancient commodity markets to its current dominance in the world of modern financial markets, price action trading has traversed epochs to become a powerful and widely utilized trading method.

1.3 Advantages and Disadvantages of Price Action Trading

Price action trading presents several notable benefits, yet it also harbors certain drawbacks that warrant consideration.

Advantages

Simplicity: The primary advantage of price action trading lies in its simplicity. By focusing solely on price movements and chart patterns, traders can sidestep the complexity often associated with employing multiple technical indicators. This facilitates clearer and more direct market analysis.

Objectivity: Relying on raw price data renders price action trading notably more objective than other approaches predicated on subjective interpretations of technical indicators. Traders base decisions on chart-based observations rather than external opinions or predictions.

Adaptability: This approach proves adaptable across a spectrum of financial markets and diverse timeframes. Whether trading equities, currencies, futures, or cryptocurrencies, the tenets of price action trading remain consistent. Moreover, it accommodates both short-term and long-term trading strategies.

Responsiveness to Market Dynamics: Given its focus on recent price movements, price action trading enables traders to swiftly respond to shifts in the market. This attribute is particularly advantageous in volatile or rapidly evolving market conditions.

Limitations

Training and Practice Requisite: While the concept of price action trading is straightforward, its practical application demands a comprehensive grasp of technical analysis and consistent practice to cultivate requisite skills. Traders must adeptly recognize price patterns and interpret them accurately to inform effective trading decisions.

Susceptibility to False Signals: Similar to other analysis methodologies, price action trading is not immune to generating false signals. Price movements can be influenced by myriad factors, including economic data releases, geopolitical developments, and fluctuations in global markets, thereby complicating precise trading decisions.

Not Universally Suited: Some traders may find adherence to such a simplistic trading approach challenging, particularly if they are accustomed to employing a diverse array of technical indicators in their analysis. Each trader boasts a unique style and disposition, and what proves efficacious for one may not resonate with another.

This approach affords numerous benefits, encompassing simplicity, objectivity, and adaptability across varied markets and timeframes. Nonetheless, it is essential to recognize its limitations and appreciate that successful implementation demands ongoing training and practice.

Chapter 2: Price Chart Analysis

2.1 Using Japanese Candlesticks in Technical Analysis

Japanese candlesticks are essential tools in the arsenal of any price action trader. Their use in technical analysis provides unique insights into market behavior and enables traders to make informed decisions. As a seasoned stock market specialist with over 20 years of experience, I have observed the remarkable effectiveness of Japanese candlesticks in predicting price movements.

Origin and Significance of Japanese Candlesticks

Japanese candlesticks trace their origins back to 18th-century Japan, where they were used to track rice price movements. Each candlestick represents price action over a given period, whether it's a minute, an hour, a day, or any other time unit. Each candlestick has an upper and lower "wick," representing the period's highs and lows, respectively, and a "body" that indicates the difference between the opening and closing prices.

The color of the body (typically red for a close lower than the open and green for a close higher) provides a quick visual indication of price movement direction.
Interpretation of Candlestick Patterns
Japanese candlesticks offer a variety of patterns and configurations that provide valuable insights into market psychology. For example, a "hammer" is a candlestick with a small lower wick and a body near the highs, indicating a rejection of lower price levels and potential bullish reversal.

Other patterns, such as evening stars or morning stars, offer indications of potential trend reversals. For instance, an evening star consists of a large bullish candlestick, followed by a small bearish candlestick that opens above the previous candle's close and closes below the previous candle's body's midpoint, indicating a possible downtrend reversal.
Integration of Japanese Candlesticks into Trading Strategy
As an experienced trader, I have found that judicious use of Japanese candlesticks can significantly enhance my trading strategy.
By combining candlestick analysis with other technical analysis tools, such as trendlines and support and resistance levels, I can identify timely entry and exit points for my trades.

For example, if I spot a hammer at a key support level on a daily chart, it could be a signal to initiate a long position, with a stop-loss placed just below the hammer's low to limit losses. Similarly, if I notice an evening star at the peak of an uptrend, it could be a signal to sell, with a stop-loss placed above the evening star's high to protect potential profits.

The use of Japanese candlesticks in technical analysis is a critical skill for any price action trader. Their ability to provide insights into future price direction and potential entry and exit points makes them a valuable tool in the toolkit of any experienced trader.

2.2 Identifying Candlestick Patterns for Trading

The art of technical analysis largely relies on the ability to interpret Japanese candlestick patterns. These configurations on price charts provide crucial insights into market psychology, and accurately identifying them can be key to success for any trader. As a trading veteran, I've closely observed the significance of this skill, and I'll share insightful perspectives on its practical application with you.

Deep Understanding of Candlestick Patterns

To navigate successfully in the world of Japanese candlesticks, it's essential to grasp the meaning of each pattern. Each candlestick tells a story, and by decoding these stories, we can anticipate future price movements.

Introduction to Candlestick Patterns: Japanese candlesticks are more than mere figures on a chart. They represent battles between buyers and sellers, moments of uncertainty, and signs of market strength or weakness.

Typology of Candlesticks: Explore a variety of candlestick patterns, from classics like the "doji" to more complex ones like the "harami" or "piercing line." Each pattern has its own significance and can provide valuable clues about upcoming movements.

Practical Application of Candlestick Patterns

Theory alone isn't sufficient in the trading world. Knowing how to apply this knowledge in real markets is crucial.

Interpreting Patterns: Delve into how to correctly interpret candlestick patterns. For instance, a "hammer" after a prolonged downtrend may signal exhaustion of the bearish trend and potential reversal to the upside.

Identification on Charts: We'll examine real examples together, analyzing price charts to spot candlestick patterns and understand their impact on trading decisions.

Integration into a Holistic Trading Strategy

Using candlestick patterns isn't limited to isolated analysis. It should be integrated into a comprehensive trading strategy.

Confirmation with Other Indicators: Candlestick patterns can be powerfully confirmed by other technical indicators. We'll explore how to combine candlestick signals with other technical analysis tools to reinforce our convictions.

Risk Management: Prudent risk management is essential. We'll address best practices for placing stop-loss orders and taking profits, using candlestick patterns as a guide to limit losses and maximize gains.

Examples and Anecdotes

Let me tell you the story of a memorable day in the markets where identifying a "bullish engulfing pattern" was the turning point for a series of successful trades.

On that day, buyers overwhelmed sellers, indicating strong potential for a bullish reversal. This anecdote underscores the importance of remaining vigilant and responsive to the opportunities presented by candlestick patterns.

In summary, identifying candlestick patterns is much more than just a technical skill. It's a true art form that requires both a deep theoretical understanding and practical experience in real markets.

MARUBOZU

HARAMI

HAMMER

2.3 Using Trendlines in Chart Analysis

In the realm of trading, trendlines are essential tools for analyzing price movements and identifying market trends. As a seasoned expert in stocks and investments, I'll delve deeper into the practical use of trendlines in chart analysis.

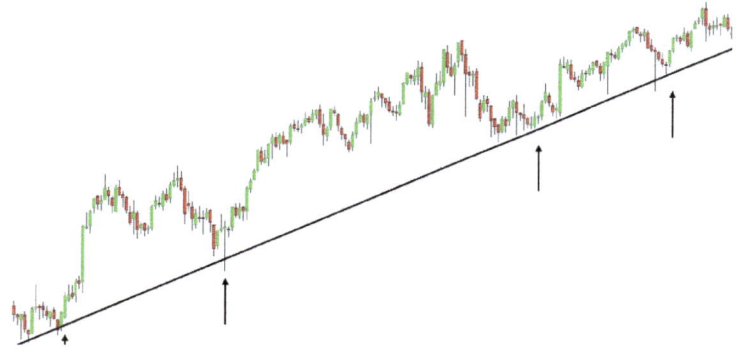

Understanding Trendlines

Definition and Basics:

Trendlines are straight lines that connect two significant points on a chart, either highs (in a downtrend) or lows (in an uptrend). They provide a visual indication of the overall market direction.

Types of Trendlines:

We can distinguish several types of trendlines based on the direction of the trend they represent. Upward trendlines are drawn by connecting two successive lows, indicating an uptrend. Conversely, downward trendlines are drawn by connecting two successive highs, indicating a downtrend.

Practical Application of Trendlines

Identification and Drawing:

To draw an effective trendline, it's crucial to select relevant connection points. Ideally, these points should be clearly visible and aligned with the overall market trend. The more contact points with the trendline, the more it's considered valid.

Interpreting Breakouts:

Breakouts from trendlines are significant events that can indicate a potential change in market dynamics. A breakout above a downward trendline or below an upward trendline may signal a trend reversal or an acceleration of the existing trend.

Integration into a Trading Strategy

Confirmation with Other Indicators:

Trendlines can be confirmed by other technical indicators such as moving averages or oscillators. For example, a breakout from a downward trendline accompanied by bullish divergence on an oscillator could strengthen the bullish reversal signal.

Risk Management:

When using trendlines to make trading decisions, it's essential to implement rigorous risk management. This involves placing stop-loss orders at appropriate levels to limit losses in case of adverse market movements.

Trendlines are powerful tools in a trader's arsenal. Proper use can provide valuable insights into market trends and help traders make informed decisions. By integrating trendlines into a comprehensive trading strategy and confirming them with

2.4 Finding Support and Resistance Levels

Finding support and resistance levels is a crucial aspect of technical analysis in trading, regardless of your level of experience. Whether you're new to trading or a seasoned expert, understanding how to identify these key levels on charts can make all the difference in your success in financial markets.

Let me guide you through this exploration, tailoring my explanations to meet the needs and knowledge of everyone.

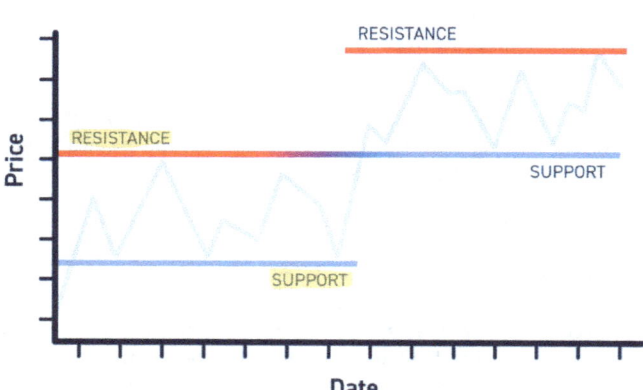

Understanding Support and Resistance Levels

Support levels are like floors where prices tend to bounce, while resistance levels act as ceilings where prices struggle to climb. Imagine yourself in a house: support is the solid ground beneath you, while resistance is the ceiling above you that prevents you from going higher.

These levels are areas where supply and demand balance out, creating potential reversal points in price movement. Support and resistance levels are often determined by previous prices where the market has reacted significantly, whether by bouncing or stagnating.

Methods for Finding Support and Resistance Levels

Finding these levels can start with a simple observation of historical charts. Spot where prices have bounced or stagnated several times in the past. These areas often indicate potential support and resistance levels.

For Experts: In addition to direct chart observation, technical indicators such as Fibonacci retracements, pivot points, and Fibonacci levels can be used to identify these key levels. These tools can provide additional validation of identified support and resistance levels.

Practical Application in Trading

Once you've identified these levels on a chart, observe how the market reacts when prices approach these areas. If prices bounce strongly near a support level or encounter strong resistance near a resistance level, it can confirm the validity of these levels.

For Experts: Use these support and resistance levels as reference points for making trading decisions. Consider entering a long position near support with a stop-loss just below it, or taking profits near resistance with a nearby profit target.

Practical Example:

Let's say you're tracking the price of a particular stock in the stock market. You notice that prices have bounced several times around a key support level, located around $50. At the same time, you identify a resistance level at about $65, where prices struggle to surpass.

By observing price action near these levels, you see that whenever prices approach $50, buyers seem to step in, causing a significant bounce. Similarly, when prices reach $65, sellers come into play, limiting any further rise.

Using these levels as guides, you might consider buying near support at $50 with a stop-loss just below it, or selling near resistance at $65 with a nearby profit target.

Whether you're a novice or an expert trader, finding support and resistance levels is a crucial skill to master.

Chapter 3: Trend Identification

3.1 Using Moving Averages to Identify Trends

Moving averages are indispensable tools in a trader's arsenal, providing an efficient way to identify trends in financial markets. In this subchapter, we will delve deeply into how moving averages work, their practical use in identifying trends, factors to consider when using them, application examples, and practical tips to maximize their effectiveness.

Introduction to Moving Averages

Moving averages are technical indicators that smooth price data over a specific period. Unlike raw prices, which can be volatile and subject to erratic movements, moving averages offer a clearer and smoother view of price evolution. Identifying trends is essential in trading as it enables traders to make informed decisions about buying or selling financial assets.

How Moving Averages Work

Moving averages are calculated by taking the average of prices over a specific period. For example, a 50-day moving average is calculated by averaging the closing prices of the last 50 trading days. This average is then plotted on the chart, creating a smooth line that represents the overall price trend over that period.

There are several types of moving averages, including simple, exponential, and weighted moving averages. Each of these calculation methods has its advantages and disadvantages, but they are all widely used in technical analysis to identify trends in financial markets.

Practical Use of Moving Averages

Moving averages are primarily used to identify trends in financial markets. When the short-term moving average crosses above the long-term moving average, it generally indicates the start of an uptrend. Similarly, a crossover below can signal the beginning of a downtrend.

However, it's important not to rely solely on moving average crossovers to make trading decisions. It's best to use them in conjunction with other technical indicators and in-depth market analysis to confirm trends and avoid false signals.

Factors to Consider

When using moving averages to identify trends, it's essential to consider several factors. The sensitivity of moving averages to the chosen periods is important because too short periods can result in false signals, while too long periods can delay signals.

It's also important to validate moving average signals with other technical indicators, such as support and resistance levels, oscillators, or trading volumes. This cross-validation can help confirm trends and reduce the risk of making decisions based on false signals.

Application Examples

We will analyze how moving average crossovers can be used to identify uptrends and downtrends, as well as when it's best to enter or exit a trading position.

Imagine we are looking at the price chart of stock ABC over a one-year period. We have plotted two moving averages: a 50-day moving average (MMA50) and a 200-day moving average (MMA200).

Identifying Uptrend:

At the beginning of the year, we observe that MMA50 crosses above MMA200, indicating a bullish crossover signal. This suggests that the short-term trend is becoming stronger than the long-term trend, which may signal the start of an uptrend.

Confirmation of Uptrend:

Subsequently, we see that prices continue to rise, with the MMA50 curve staying above MMA200. This confirmation of the uptrend reinforces our conviction in the strength of the long-term trend.

Entry Point:

A potential entry point could be identified when prices retraced slightly towards MMA50 but then bounced, thus confirming the continuation of the uptrend. Traders might consider entering a long position at this point, anticipating a continuation of the uptrend.

Exit Point:

To determine a potential exit point, traders could monitor a crossover of MMA50 below MMA200. This crossover would indicate a weakening of the uptrend and could be interpreted as a signal to exit the long position.

Identifying Downtrend:

Later in the year, we observe that MMA50 crosses below MMA200, signaling a bearish crossover. This suggests a change in market dynamics, with the short-term trend becoming weaker than the long-term trend, potentially indicating the start of a downtrend.

By using these moving average crossover signals, traders can identify uptrends and downtrends in the market and make informed trading decisions regarding entry and exit points of their positions. However, it's important to remember that moving averages are not infallible and should be used in conjunction with other technical analysis tools and proper risk management.

Practical Tips

To maximize the effectiveness of moving averages in trend identification, here are some practical tips to follow:

- Use multiple periods of moving averages to confirm trends.
- Adjust the periods of moving averages based on market volatility.
- Validate moving average signals with other technical indicators.
- Do not rely solely on moving average crossovers to make trading decisions.

By following these tips, you can use moving averages more effectively in your trend analysis and make more informed and profitable trading decisions.

Conclusion

Moving averages are valuable tools in any trader's toolbox, offering a simple yet powerful method to identify trends in financial markets.

By understanding their operation, practical use, factors to consider, application examples, and practical tips, you can improve your ability to identify and exploit trends in financial markets, thereby increasing your chances of success in trading.

3.2 Recognizing Trends with Highs and Lows Analysis

Analyzing highs and lows is a fundamental method for recognizing trends in financial markets. It is based on the principle that prices move in cycles of highs and lows, reflecting the forces of supply and demand. In this subchapter, we will explore this approach in detail, emphasizing its relevance in trend identification and providing concrete examples to illustrate its practical application.

1. Importance of Highs and Lows Analysis

Analyzing highs and lows is crucial for traders as it provides key insights into future price direction. By identifying levels where prices have reached peaks or troughs, traders can better understand market dynamics and anticipate upcoming trends. This method offers valuable insight into market psychology and enables traders to make informed decisions.

2. Identification of Highs and Lows

To recognize trends using highs and lows analysis, traders carefully examine the peaks and troughs of price movements on a chart. Peaks represent the highest levels reached by prices, while troughs represent the lowest levels. By drawing trend lines through these levels, traders can visualize emerging trends and make informed trading decisions.

3. Types of Trends

Highs and lows analysis allows for the identification of three main types of trends:

- Uptrend: Characterized by successively higher highs and lows.
- Downtrend: Characterized by successively lower highs and lows.
- Sideways or Consolidation Trend: Characterized by peaks and troughs generally at similar levels, indicating a balance between supply and demand.

Recognizing these trends allows traders to adjust their trading strategy accordingly, seeking to profit from upcoming price movements.

4. Practical Use in Trading

In practice, traders use highs and lows analysis in several ways:

- Identification of Entry and Exit Points: Highs and lows levels can serve as potential entry or exit points for trading positions. For example, a trader might

look to enter a long position when prices exceed a previous high, thereby confirming an uptrend.
- Confirmation of Trends: Trend lines drawn through highs and lows can be used to confirm emerging trends. An uptrend can be confirmed by a series of higher highs, while a downtrend can be confirmed by a series of lower lows.
- Anticipation of Trend Reversals: Traders can use highs and lows analysis to anticipate potential trend reversals. For example, a trend reversal to the upside might be signaled by a high lower than the previous one, indicating possible weakness in the current trend.

5. Application Examples

To illustrate the practical application of highs and lows analysis in trading, let's examine a concrete example:

On a price chart of a stock, traders identify a series of successively higher highs and higher lows, thus confirming an uptrend. By drawing a trend line through these highs and lows, traders can visualize the overall market direction and make trading decisions accordingly.

6. Tips for Accurate Trend Recognition

To accurately recognize trends using highs and lows analysis, here are some practical tips:

- Use Multiple Time Frames: To confirm trends at different levels of granularity, use multiple time frames in your analysis.
- Pay Attention to Breakouts: Breakouts of highs and lows levels can indicate changes in market direction.
- Use Other Indicators: Use other technical indicators to confirm signals generated by highs and lows analysis.

By following these tips, you can use highs and lows analysis more effectively in your trend analysis and make more informed and profitable trading decisions.

3.3 Trend Confirmation Using Supplementary Indicators

Confirming trends using supplementary indicators is a crucial step in the technical analysis process. While analyzing highs and lows provides valuable insight into the overall market direction, using additional indicators helps validate these trends and improve the reliability of trading signals. In this subchapter, we will explore the different categories of supplementary indicators, their practical use in trend confirmation, and provide concrete examples to illustrate their application in trading.

1. Categories of Supplementary Indicators

Supplementary indicators can be grouped into several categories, including:

- Momentum Indicators: These indicators measure the strength and speed of price movements, which can help confirm emerging trends.
- Oscillators: These indicators typically oscillate between predefined levels, indicating overbought or oversold market conditions.
- Volume: Analyzing trading volume can provide insights into investor participation and the validity of price movements.
- Volatility: Volatility indicators measure the magnitude of price fluctuations, which can help assess the risk associated with a given trend.

2. Practical Use of Supplementary Indicators

Practical use of supplementary indicators is crucial for confirming emerging trends and making informed trading decisions. Here are specific tips for effective use of these indicators:

Understanding the Strengths and Weaknesses of Each Indicator:

- Before using an indicator, take the time to understand its characteristics, parameters, and limitations. Each indicator has its own strengths and weaknesses, and it's essential to know them to avoid common pitfalls.

Establishing Clear Rules for Interpreting Signals:

- Develop clear rules for interpreting signals generated by the indicators. For example, set specific thresholds for overbought and oversold readings in oscillators, or criteria for line crossovers in momentum indicators.

Confirming Signals through Indicator Convergence:

- Look for cross-confirmations using multiple supp
- lementary indicators. For example, if you use the RSI to identify overbought or oversold conditions, also look for trend reversal signals in other indicators like MACD or Stochastic.

Adapting to Changing Market Conditions:

- Be flexible in your use of indicators and adapt to changing market conditions. What works well in a trending market may not be as effective in a ranging market. Learn to adjust your indicator parameters or use different combinations based on current market conditions.

Regular Evaluation of Indicator Effectiveness:

- Regularly assess the effectiveness of your indicators to ensure they continue to provide reliable signals. If an indicator isn't performing as expected or is generating too many false signals, be prepared to adjust it or replace it with a more suitable indicator.

3. Application Examples

To illustrate the practical application of supplementary indicators in trading, consider a concrete example:

On a price chart of a stock, a trader observes an uptrend confirmed by a series of successively higher highs and higher lows. To validate this trend, the trader uses the Stochastic indicator to identify overbought zones, confirming the strength of the uptrend.

4. Tips for Accurate Trend Confirmation

For accurately confirming trends using supplementary indicators, here are some practical tips:

Choose Compatible Indicators:

- Use indicators that complement your analysis and offer different perspectives on the market.

Avoid Indicator Overload:

- Limit the number of indicators you use to avoid confusion and analysis paralysis.

Be Patient:

- Wait for confirmation from multiple indicators before making a trading decision to minimize false signals.

Confirming trends using supplementary indicators is an essential step in the technical analysis process. By using a judicious combination of indicators, traders can validate emerging trends and improve the reliability of their trading decisions.

Chapter 4: Price Action-Based Trading Strategies

4.1 Trend Reversal Strategies

Trend reversal strategies are potent tools in a trader's toolkit, as they allow for spotting contra-trend trading opportunities when prices reach extreme levels and could potentially change direction. This section will delve deeply into different techniques and tools used to identify and confirm trend reversals, along with practical advice for traders.

In the intricate world of trading, spotting trend reversal signals requires a profound understanding of market dynamics. Here are some commonly used tools for this task:

Divergence: Divergence between technical indicators and price can indicate a weakening of the current trend. For instance, if prices continue to rise while momentum indicators like RSI (Relative Strength Index) or MACD (Moving Average Convergence Divergence) start to decline, it suggests a possible imminent trend reversal.

Candlestick Patterns: Candlestick patterns provide visual signals on price charts that can indicate a change in direction. For example, a shooting star or a inverted hammer near a significant support or resistance level may signal a potential reversal.

Fibonacci Levels: Traders often use Fibonacci retracement levels to identify zones where prices are likely to bounce after a correction. Fibonacci levels, such as 38.2%, 50%, and 61.8%, often act as support or resistance levels where trend reversals frequently occur.

Confirming trend reversal signals is essential to avoid false signals and market traps. Here are some commonly used techniques to confirm trend reversals:

Volume Analysis: An increase in trading volume during a trend reversal can confirm the validity of the price movement. For instance, high volume during the formation of a significant peak or trough reinforces the likelihood of the trend reversal being genuine.

Breakout Confirmation: Breakouts of trend lines or support/resistance levels can confirm a trend reversal. Traders often monitor these breakouts to validate their trend reversal assumptions and take positions accordingly.

To succeed in trend reversal trading, here are some additional tips to consider:

Patience and Discipline: Wait for confirmation of trend reversal signals before taking action. Avoid rushing your trading decisions and maintain discipline in your approach.

Risk Management: Use stop-loss orders to limit losses in case of an unexpected trend reversal. Also, manage your position sizes to control your market exposure.

Validation by Multiple Indicators: Use multiple indicators and techniques to validate your trend reversal hypotheses. Multiple confirmations enhance the likelihood of your trade's success.

4.2 Trend Continuation Strategies

Trend continuation strategies are crucial for traders aiming to seize trading opportunities when markets exhibit a clear direction. Unlike trend reversal strategies that target capturing changes in direction, trend continuation strategies focus on identifying moments where an existing trend is likely to persist.

In this section, we will delve into these strategies in an accessible manner, highlighting the tools and techniques used to spot and trade ongoing trends.

Identifying Trend Continuation Signals
Identifying trend continuation signals involves observing market movements to determine if a trend is likely to extend. Here are some of the tools and techniques you can employ:
Moving Averages: Moving averages help identify the general direction of a trend. When the price remains above the moving average, it indicates an uptrend, while staying below indicates a downtrend.

> Momentum Indicators: These indicators, such as the Relative Strength Index (RSI) or the Moving Average Convergence Divergence (MACD), measure the strength of a current trend. High readings suggest a strong trend that could continue.

Confirming Signals
Confirming trend continuation signals is essential to avoid false signals. Here are some simple confirmation techniques you can use:
Volume Analysis: High volume during a trend confirms its strength. Decreasing volume may indicate weakening of the trend.

Consolidation: Periods of consolidation, where prices stabilize after a strong move in the trend direction, can confirm the trend's strength.

Practical Examples

Imagine you are a trader looking for trend continuation opportunities in the currency market. You observe the daily chart of the EUR/USD currency pair, showing a well-established uptrend over the past few months. You have already identified this trend through price action analysis, which shows progressively higher highs and lows.

Upon closer analysis of the chart, you notice that the EUR/USD pair recently experienced a period of consolidation after a sharp uptrend. This is characterized by a period where prices moved sideways in a narrow range, marking a pause in the previous uptrend.

This consolidation is often considered a potential signal of trend continuation as it allows the market to catch its breath before resuming its previous momentum.

As the consolidation continues, you closely monitor key support and resistance levels. You notice that the price has bounced several times at a major support level near 1.1500, confirming the strength of this zone. Additionally, you observe that trading volume has decreased during the consolidation period, suggesting market participants are awaiting the next impulse.

Your analysis is reinforced by the technical indicators you use. The RSI shows readings in the overbought zone, confirming the strength of the current uptrend. Furthermore, the MACD presents a bullish divergence, indicating potentially increasing momentum in favor of buyers.

After considering all this information, you decide to wait for a breakout above the key resistance level near 1.1600 to confirm the continuation of the uptrend. Once this breakout occurs with high volume, confirming the strength of buyers, you decide to enter a long position on the EUR/USD.

You manage your risk by placing a stop-loss order just below the last significant low, ensuring to limit your losses in case of a sudden market reversal. You also closely monitor the progress of the uptrend, potentially adjusting your stop-loss as the price moves in your favor.

Over the following days and weeks, you observe with satisfaction as the EUR/USD pair continues to rise, confirming your initial analysis. You remain disciplined in your approach, closely following trend continuation signals and rigorously managing your position to maximize potential gains while minimizing losses.

In summary, this example illustrates how a trader can use various analysis techniques to identify and capitalize on trend continuation opportunities in the currency market.

By combining in-depth analysis of price movements, technical indicators, and support and resistance levels, you can make informed trading decisions and succeed in capitalizing on evolving market trends.
Tips for Trend Continuation Trading
Follow the Trend: The trend is your friend. Seek to trade in the direction of the dominant trend to increase your chances of success.
Be Patient: Wait for confirmation of trend continuation signals before making a trading decision. Patience is often rewarded in trading.

Manage your Risks: Always use stop-loss orders to limit your losses in case of adverse market movements. Also, manage position size to control your market exposure.

4.3 Trading Based on Fibonacci Retracements

Fibonacci retracements are a popular tool used by many traders to identify potential levels of support and resistance on a chart. These levels are derived from mathematical ratios based on the Fibonacci sequence and are often used to anticipate trend reversals or consolidation areas in financial markets.

Here's how this strategy can be effectively implemented:

Understanding Fibonacci Retracements:

> Before you can use Fibonacci retracements in your trading, it is essential to understand how they are calculated and interpreted. The most commonly used retracement levels are 23.6%, 38.2%, 50%, 61.8%, and 78.6%, which are considered potential support or resistance zones.

Identification of Retracements on a Chart:

> Once you have understood Fibonacci retracement levels, you can use them to identify potential trend reversal or consolidation areas on a chart. Look for retracements that correspond to significant previous lows or highs, as these areas are more likely to attract the attention of other traders.
> Confirmation of Retracements:

Using Combinations of Retracements:

- Instead of relying solely on one Fibonacci retracement level, traders can use multiple retracement levels to confirm the validity of a support or resistance zone. The convergence of several retracements, such as the 50% retracement with the 61.8% retracement, strengthens the solidity of the identified zone.

Validation through Market Context Analysis:

- It is crucial to analyze the overall market context to confirm Fibonacci retracements. For example, a Fibonacci retracement coinciding with a historical support level or a major market pivot has a higher probability of being valid.

Confirmation through Volatility Analysis:

- Market volatility can provide insights into the strength or weakness of a Fibonacci retracement. High volatility near a retracement level may indicate significant buyer or seller pressure, thus confirming the validity of the identified zone.

Using Statistical Validation Methods:

- Some traders use statistical techniques to validate Fibonacci retracement levels. For example, analyzing the historical probability of bouncing from certain retracement levels can provide insights into the reliability of these levels in similar market conditions.

Risk Management:

- As always, prudent risk management is essential when trading based on Fibonacci retracements. Use stop-loss orders to limit losses in case of adverse movements and ensure you adhere to your risk management plan for each transaction.

Concrete Example:
Suppose you are observing the chart of a currency pair that has recently experienced a strong uptrend. You notice that the price begins to retrace a portion of this trend and approaches the 50% Fibonacci retracement level.
You patiently wait for the price to reach this retracement level and carefully observe the market's reaction. You notice that the price begins to bounce near the 50% retracement level, suggesting buyer interest at this level.

Taking this observation into account, along with other confirmation factors such as trend reversal signals or candlestick patterns, you decide to enter a long position on the currency pair. You manage your risk by placing a stop-loss order just below the Fibonacci retracement level, ensuring you limit your losses in case of a market reversal.

Over time, the price of the currency pair does indeed bounce from the Fibonacci retracement level and resumes its uptrend, confirming the validity of your analysis. You closely monitor the trend's progress and adjust your stop-loss if necessary to protect your gains.

By using Fibonacci retracements as a guide, you have been able to identify a potentially lucrative trading opportunity and capitalize on the trend reversal in the currency market. This example illustrates how this strategy can be effectively implemented in real trading.

4.4 Managing Entry and Exit Positions

Utilizing Advanced Technical Analysis:

> Advanced technical analysis is a crucial component of managing entry and exit positions, providing traders with sophisticated tools to make informed decisions in the market. Here are some advanced technical analysis techniques and their application in managing entry and exit positions:

a. Specific Candlestick Patterns:

Candlestick patterns offer a wealth of information on price behavior and can provide valuable insights into entry and exit points. For instance, patterns like the morning star, evening star, inverted hammer, gravestone doji, etc., often signal potential trend reversals. By analyzing these patterns contextually, considering support and resistance levels, as well as longer-term trends, traders can identify trading opportunities with a favorable risk-to-reward ratio.

b. Recognition of Complex Chart Patterns:

In addition to simple candlestick patterns, traders can turn to more complex chart patterns to refine their entry and exit positions. For example, patterns such as triangles, flags, pennants, head and shoulders, etc., offer insights into consolidation and trend continuation phases in the market. By accurately identifying and interpreting these patterns, traders can anticipate future price movements and make more informed trading decisions.

c. Interpretation of Advanced Oscillator Signals:

Oscillators like the Relative Strength Index (RSI), Moving Average Convergence Divergence (MACD), and Stochastic Oscillator provide information about trend strength and direction. Traders can use specific configurations of these indicators to confirm entry and exit points. For example, a divergence between the RSI and prices may indicate a weakening of the current trend, while a signal line crossover on the MACD may signal an imminent trend reversal. By interpreting these signals accurately and combining them with other technical analyses, traders can improve their timing of entry and exit and optimize their trading performance.

Utilizing Confirmation Signals:

> Using confirmation signals is essential to validate entry decisions. This may involve using technical indicators such as moving averages, Bollinger Bands, or stochastic oscillators to confirm potential entry points. For instance, if you are considering buying a stock, you may wait for the price to exceed its moving average over a given period, which may indicate increased bullish momentum.

Risk Management:

> Risk management is the cornerstone of any successful trading strategy. It involves assessing and controlling the risks associated with each transaction to protect invested capital. Here are some key risk management principles that every trader should consider:

a. Determining the acceptable risk level: Before entering a position, it is essential to determine the amount of capital you are willing to risk on a single trade. This decision depends on your risk tolerance, investment horizon, and financial goals. Generally, it is recommended not to risk more than 1 to 2% of your total capital on a single transaction.

b. Using stop-loss orders: Stop-loss orders are essential tools for limiting losses in case of adverse market movements. By setting an appropriate stop-loss level before entering a position, you can determine in advance the amount of loss you are willing to accept. It is important to place your stop-loss at a level that protects you against normal market fluctuations while avoiding being triggered by random price movements.

c. Portfolio diversification: Portfolio diversification is an effective strategy to reduce the overall risk of your portfolio.

By investing in a variety of assets and asset classes, you can spread your risk exposure and mitigate the impact of extreme market movements on your overall capital. It is recommended to diversify your portfolio among different stocks, currencies, commodities, and bonds, as well as to use instruments such as ETFs and index funds to increase diversification.

d. Continuous monitoring and adjustments: Risk management is not limited to setting initial stop-loss levels. It is essential to actively monitor your open positions and adjust your stop-loss orders based on market developments. If the price moves in your favor, you may consider moving your stop-loss to secure your gains.

Likewise, if the market moves against you, you should be prepared to cut your losses quickly to limit damage.

Active Monitoring:

> Active market monitoring is necessary once you are in a position. Carefully monitor price movements and adjust your stop-loss and take-profit orders based on new information and market developments.
> For example, if significant economic news is released, it may affect market conditions and warrant an adjustment of your orders.

Exit Planning:

> Determine your profit targets and the conditions under which you intend to exit the position in advance. Use techniques such as support and resistance level analysis, as well as identification of potential reversal points, to set your exit goals.
> This can help you make informed decisions and avoid letting emotions dictate your actions.

Post-Trade Evaluation:

> After closing a position, take the time to evaluate your performance. Analyze what worked well and what did not, and draw lessons from each trade. Identify your strengths and weaknesses, and use this information to refine your trading strategy in the future.
> Continuous learning is essential to improve your trading skills and increase your long-term profitability.

Chapter 5: Risk and Money Management

5.1 Significance of Risk Management in Trading

In the realm of trading, risk management is much more than just a practice; it's a vital necessity for any serious trader. Understanding and implementing effective risk management is key to preserving one's capital and maintaining stable long-term growth in the financial markets. In this chapter, we will delve deep into the crucial importance of risk management in trading.

Firstly, risk management is fundamental to safeguarding a trader's initial capital. Every trader embarks on their journey with a certain amount of capital that they invest in the markets. Without proper risk management, this capital is exposed to significant potential losses.

Indeed, financial markets are inherently volatile and unpredictable, meaning sudden and adverse price movements can occur at any time. By applying risk management techniques such as using stop-loss orders and determining an appropriate position size, traders can limit their potential losses to a manageable level, thus preserving their capital for future trading opportunities.

Secondly, effective risk management helps minimize the negative effects of emotions on trading. Financial markets are often subject to fluctuations and periods of volatility, which can trigger emotional reactions in traders, such as fear, greed, or stress. These emotions can often lead to impulsive or irrational decisions that go against a well-thought-out trading strategy.

By adopting a disciplined approach to risk management, traders can mitigate the effects of these fluctuations by focusing on clear strategies and objectives rather than their emotions. This enables them to make rational, fact-based decisions, which is essential for maintaining consistent trading performance over the long term.

Finally, effective risk management allows traders to maintain a sustainable approach to trading. By limiting losses and protecting their capital, traders can continue to trade profitably even in the face of challenging market periods. This enables them to stay in the market longer, continuously learn and improve, and ultimately achieve their long-term financial goals.

In summary, risk management is a fundamental pillar of successful trading. By understanding and applying the principles of risk management, traders can protect their capital, manage their emotions, and maintain a sustainable approach to trading.

This maximizes their chances of success in the financial markets and helps them achieve their long-term financial goals.

5.2 Determining the Appropriate Position Size

Calculation of the optimal position size:

Kelly Criterion Method: This method, developed by mathematician John L. Kelly Jr., is based on information theory and aims to maximize exponential capital growth over the long term. It takes into account the probability of gain and loss for each trade, as well as the risk-reward ratio. The goal is to determine the optimal fraction of capital to risk on each trade to achieve maximum returns.

Percentage of Capital Method: This approach involves allocating a fixed percentage of the total capital to each trade, regardless of the specific risk associated with it. For example, a trader may decide to allocate 2% of their capital to each trade. This method is simple to implement but does not consider differences in risk between trades.

Adapting position size to market volatility:

Understanding how to adjust risk exposure based on changing market conditions is essential for traders, requiring a thorough understanding of techniques for adapting position size to volatility.

Using the Average True Range (ATR):

The Average True Range (ATR) is a valuable tool for assessing market volatility. This measure provides an estimate of the average price range over a given period. Traders often use it to determine position size based on the current market volatility. For example, if the ATR indicates high volatility, traders may reduce their position size to limit their risk exposure. Conversely, when volatility is low, they may increase their position size to capitalize on trading opportunities in a more stable market.

Proportional adjustment techniques:

Proportional adjustment techniques allow traders to adapt their position size in proportion to market volatility. For example, some traders use a fixed ratio between the ATR and their position size. If the ATR increases, the position size decreases proportionally, and vice versa. This approach enables traders to maintain a consistent level of risk relative to market volatility.

Adapting to market conditions:

Traders must be aware of market conditions and adjust their position size accordingly. In a highly volatile market, price movements can be more unpredictable, increasing the risk for traders. By reducing their position size, traders can limit their risk exposure. Conversely, in a calmer market, trading opportunities may be less frequent but more predictable. Traders can then increase their position size to take advantage of these opportunities.

Dynamic risk management:

Dynamic risk management involves continuously adjusting position size based on market fluctuations. Some traders use algorithms or automated strategies to monitor market volatility and automatically adjust their position size accordingly. For example, a trader may set predefined volatility thresholds and adjust their position size when these thresholds are exceeded. This allows for proactive risk management and quick adaptation to market changes.

Dynamic risk management: It is crucial to adjust position size based on market volatility to preserve capital and avoid excessive losses. For example, in a highly volatile market, it may be necessary to reduce position size to limit risk exposure. Conversely, in a less volatile market, a larger position size may be justified to maximize profit opportunities.

Position size adjustment techniques: Traders can use a variety of techniques to adjust position size based on market volatility. This can include using a fixed position size per unit of volatility, where position size is proportional to price movement. Alternatively, traders may use specific rules based on volatility indicators such as the Average True Range (ATR) to determine the appropriate position size.

Adjustment based on confidence in the strategy:

Evaluation of confidence in the strategy: Traders must objectively assess their confidence in a trading strategy based on tangible criteria such as past performance, the robustness of the strategy in different market conditions, and the consistency of results. Excessive confidence can lead to overexposure to risk, while underestimating confidence can result in underutilization of trading opportunities.

Risks of overexposure: Overexposure to risk can result from excessive confidence in a strategy or a series of successful trades. It is essential to maintain a disciplined approach and adhere to risk management principles, even when confidence in a trading opportunity is high. This helps prevent significant losses in the event of a market reversal or a series of losing trades.

5.3 Utilization of Stop-loss and Take-profit Orders

Stop-loss Orders

Stop-loss orders are essential for any cautious and well-thought-out trading strategy. They serve to cap losses by setting a predetermined level at which a position must be automatically closed if the market moves unfavorably. Here's a detailed exploration of the strategic use of stop-loss orders:

a. Definition and Functioning

A stop-loss order is an automatic sell instruction placed at a defined price level below the entry price for a long position, or above the entry price for a short position. When this level is reached or exceeded, the order is executed, thus closing the position and limiting potential losses.

b. Importance of Stop-loss Orders

Stop-loss orders are crucial for safeguarding a trader's capital against unexpected and excessive market movements. By setting a predefined exit level, traders can control their risk and avoid catastrophic losses that could jeopardize their trading account.

c. Strategic Placement

To determine the optimal protection level for a position, several factors need consideration, including market volatility, position duration, technical analysis, and position size relative to the trader's total capital. By combining these factors, traders can strategically place their stop-loss orders to effectively manage their risk.

Stop Management

Managing stop-loss orders goes beyond simply defining specific price levels for automatic position exits. Advanced strategies such as dynamically adjusting stop-loss levels based on market conditions and using trailing stop-losses can help traders better control their risk exposure and optimize their results.

Additionally, applying principles of money management is crucial for determining the appropriate size of stop-loss orders, considering available capital and the acceptable risk level for each transaction.

Impact Illustration

To illustrate the importance of stop-loss orders, let's consider a scenario where a trader decides not to use stops and incurs a series of significant losses due to unexpected market movements. This scenario highlights the crucial need for stop-loss orders to protect capital and ensure a disciplined approach to trading.

In conclusion, stop-loss orders are an indispensable tool for any serious trader. Their strategic use enables risk control, capital protection, and a disciplined trading approach. By fully understanding their functioning and incorporating them into their trading strategy, traders can enhance their overall performance and maximize their chances of success in the financial markets.

5.4 Techniques to Minimize Losses and Maximize Profits

Dynamic Management of Stop-loss and Take-profit Orders:

Let's begin with the fundamental importance of these orders. The stop-loss serves as your first line of defense against excessive losses. It sets a price level at which your position will be automatically liquidated if the market moves against you, thus limiting your losses to a predetermined amount and preserving your capital for other trading opportunities.

Similarly, the take-profit is your means of locking in gains by setting a price level at which you want to exit your position with a profit. This allows you to capture favorable price movements and achieve your profit objectives.

To strategically place these orders, you must consider several factors. First, carefully analyze the market and identify key support and resistance levels, as well as dominant trends.

Then, determine your risk tolerance and set stop-loss and take-profit levels accordingly. Ensure these levels are logical relative to market structure and your trading strategy. I also recommend using advanced techniques to dynamically adjust your orders based on changing market conditions.

For example, you can use trailing stop-losses that automatically follow the price at a fixed distance, allowing you to protect your gains while leaving room for the position to develop. Similarly, using trailing take-profit orders allows you to lock in profits while allowing the trade to continue operating in a favorable trend. Finally, remain flexible and adapt your orders as the market evolves.

If conditions change and your initial analysis is no longer valid, don't hesitate to adjust your stop-loss and take-profit levels accordingly. The key is to remain disciplined and stick to your trading plan, even when things get turbulent in the markets.

Utilization of Fundamental Analysis to Optimize Exits:

In addition to technical analysis, fundamental analysis can provide insights into economic events and market developments that could impact prices. Traders can use this information to make informed decisions about exiting their positions, either exiting before major announcements or extending their positions based on favorable outlooks.

Portfolio Diversification:

A fundamental strategy to reduce losses is portfolio diversification. By spreading capital across different assets or financial instruments, traders can mitigate risks associated with a single position or sector. This can also help maximize profit opportunities by exploiting different trends in the markets.

Prudent Leverage Usage:

While leverage can amplify gains, it also comes with significant risks. Experienced traders know when and how to use leverage prudently, avoiding taking positions that are too large relative to their capital. Prudent leverage management is essential to reduce potential losses and preserve capital.

Strategies to Maximize Profits:

Maximizing profits is a critical aspect of successful trading. In this section, I will explore different strategies and techniques to help you optimize your gains in the financial markets.

a-Managing Winning Positions:

One of the first strategies to maximize profits is effectively managing winning positions. Too often, traders tend to close their positions too early out of fear of seeing gains evaporate. However, by adopting a more disciplined approach, you can let your winning positions run when the trend is strong. This involves closely monitoring market developments and adjusting your stop-loss and take-profit orders accordingly to protect your gains while allowing enough room to capitalize on favorable price movements.

b-Utilizing Multiple Profit Targets:

Another effective strategy is using multiple profit targets. Instead of aiming for a single profit-taking level, divide your position into several parts and set different take-profit levels for each segment. This allows you to secure gains at different price levels and maximize potential profits. You can adjust these levels based on market volatility and trend strength to make the most of price movements.

c-Taking Partial Profits:

Taking partial profits is another important technique for maximizing profits. Instead of fully closing a position as soon as you reach a target profit level, you can choose to close a portion of your position and let the rest run. This allows you to lock in some gains while giving the remaining profits a chance to grow. You can use specific criteria, such as support or resistance levels, to decide when to take partial profits.

d-Optimizing Risk/Reward Ratio:

Optimizing the risk/reward ratio of your trades is also crucial to maximizing profits. This means seeking trading opportunities that offer a high potential for gain relative to the risk incurred. You can use technical analysis techniques to identify trading setups with a favorable risk/reward ratio, such as breakouts of support or resistance levels, or Japanese candlestick patterns. By focusing your efforts on trades with a good risk/reward ratio, you increase your chances of realizing profits in the long run.

e-Preserving Capital:

Finally, capital preservation is a crucial element of profit maximization. This means being cautious in managing your risk and knowing when to stay out of the market when conditions are not favorable. By using stop-loss orders to limit losses and avoiding over-trading when opportunities are unclear, you can preserve your capital for more opportune trades.

By integrating these profit-maximizing strategies into your trading approach, you will be better equipped to capitalize on opportunities in the financial markets and achieve your profitability goals.

Continuous Market Monitoring:

Finally, experienced traders know that continuous market monitoring is essential to reducing losses and maximizing profits. They remain vigilant to changes in market conditions, economic events, and significant announcements that could affect their positions. This allows them to quickly adjust their strategies and orders based on new information, minimizing risks and capitalizing on opportunities.

Chapter 6: Trading Psychology

6.1 Emotional Control and Discipline in Trading

Emotional control and discipline are the fundamental pillars upon which all success in trading rests. As an experienced trader, I have repeatedly observed the significant impact these two elements have on traders' performance in the financial markets. Here's a deeper exploration of the importance of emotional control and discipline, along with techniques to effectively develop them.

Importance of Emotional Control:

In the volatile realm of trading, emotions can quickly take over and hinder our trading decisions. Fear, greed, hope, and regret are pervasive emotions that can influence our choices and steer us away from our pre-established strategy. Emotional control involves keeping these emotions in check, acknowledging them but not allowing them to dictate our actions in the markets.

Traders who manage to maintain a calm and rational mindset are better equipped to make informed decisions and avoid emotional pitfalls that can lead to significant losses.

Development of Discipline:

Discipline is the ability to stick to one's trading plan and adhere to established rules, even in the toughest times. This entails setting clear trading goals, establishing strict risk management rules, and consistently sticking to them. Discipline is what enables traders to remain true to their trading strategy even when things get tough in the markets. Without discipline, it's easy to succumb to the temptation to deviate from the initial plan, which can result in significant losses and financial setbacks.

Techniques to Improve Emotional Control:

There are several techniques that can help traders enhance their emotional control. Meditation and mindfulness are powerful practices that aid in calming the mind and reducing stress. Positive visualization is another effective technique that allows traders to focus on their goals and bolster their self-confidence.

By establishing structured trading routines and eliminating distractions, traders can also help maintain a calm and focused mindset during trading sessions.

Management of Negative Emotions:

In the realm of trading, managing emotions is crucial to maintaining rigorous discipline and making rational trading decisions. In price action-based trading, where decisions are often made based on observed price movements on charts, emotional management is particularly important.

Recognition of Emotions:

The first step in emotional management in trading is recognizing them. Traders must be aware of the emotions that influence their decisions, such as fear of losing money, greed for bigger profits, or impatience during price consolidation periods. By identifying these emotions, traders can better understand how they affect their behavior.

Understanding Triggers:

Once emotions are recognized, it's important to understand what triggers them. For example, a trader might feel fear when experiencing a series of losses, or greed when witnessing a strong trend forming. By understanding the factors that trigger their emotions, traders can anticipate and better control their reactions.

Development of Coping Mechanisms:

Traders need to develop mechanisms to effectively manage their emotions while trading. This may include deep breathing techniques to reduce stress, regular breaks to refocus, or establishing strict risk management rules to limit the emotional impact of losses.

Maintaining Discipline:

Discipline is essential to avoid letting emotions dictate trading decisions. Traders must follow their trading plan rigorously, focusing on executing predefined strategies rather than their momentary emotions. This sometimes involves making tough decisions, such as cutting a losing position or taking profits prematurely, based on objective criteria rather than emotional reactions.

Self-Assessment and Continuous Improvement:

Finally, traders should regularly assess their own emotional behavior and identify areas where improvements can be made. This may require keeping a trading journal to track emotional reactions to different market situations and adjusting emotional management strategies accordingly.

In summary, emotional management is a fundamental aspect of price action trading. By recognizing, understanding, and effectively managing their emotions, traders can improve their discipline, reduce emotional errors, and increase their chances of success in the financial markets.

By acknowledging fears and learning to manage them, you can enhance your self-confidence and your ability to make informed decisions in the financial markets.

6.2: Stress and Anxiety Management in Trading

In this chapter, we will address the crucial aspect of managing stress and anxiety associated with trading. Trading can be a highly stressful and emotional activity, and it is essential to develop strategies to cope with these challenges. Here are some key points we will explore:

Understanding Stress Causes:

Understanding the causes of stress is the first essential step in learning to manage it effectively in the context of trading. Here's a detailed examination of the main sources of stress traders face:

Financial Pressure:

Financial pressure is one of the primary sources of stress for many traders. The idea of risking hard-earned capital in the market can generate anxiety, especially when results do not meet expectations.

Market Volatility:

Market volatility can also be a major source of stress. Financial markets can be unpredictable and experience sudden and dramatic movements, which can provoke anxiety in traders who fear significant losses.

Fear of Failure:

The fear of failure is another common stress factor among traders. The fear of making wrong decisions or experiencing losses can lead to paralysis and hesitation, which can hinder trading performance.

Sense of Loss of Control:

The feeling of loss of control is another significant source of stress. Traders may feel overwhelmed by market events and find themselves reacting excessively or irrationally, leading to costly mistakes.

Emotional Factors:

Lastly, emotional factors such as anxiety, anger, frustration, and impatience can all contribute to stress in traders. These emotions can be triggered by significant losses, periods of market stagnation, or unexpected events.

Stress Management Techniques:

Deep Breathing Practice:

Deep breathing is one of the simplest and most effective techniques for reducing stress. Traders can take a few minutes before and during the trading session to focus on their breathing, slowly inhaling through the nose, holding their breath for a few moments, and then exhaling slowly through the mouth. This can help calm the nervous system and reduce stress levels.

Regular Physical Exercise:

Regular physical exercise is an excellent way to reduce stress and promote overall well-being. Traders can integrate exercise sessions into their daily routine to help release tension and maintain a positive mindset. This can include activities such as walking, running, yoga, or meditation.

Time Management:

Poor time management can contribute to stress in traders. It is important to establish a structured trading routine and set clear limits for screen time. Traders can also plan regular breaks to rest and relax, which can help maintain their energy levels and concentration.

Relaxation Techniques:

Relaxation techniques such as meditation, guided visualization, and yoga can be extremely beneficial for reducing stress and promoting mental clarity. Traders can incorporate these practices into their daily routine to help calm the mind and stay focused during trading.

Development of Emotion Management Strategies:

Learning to recognize and manage emotions is essential for reducing trading-related stress. Traders can use techniques such as emotion journaling, acceptance and mindfulness practice, and seeking a coach or mentor to help them develop effective strategies for managing the emotional ups and downs of trading.

Establishment of Realistic Goals:

Setting realistic and achievable trading goals can help reduce stress by eliminating excessive pressure to perform. Traders can focus on continuously improving their skills and discipline rather than setting unrealistic profit goals or seeking excessive short-term gains. With clear goals, traders can better manage pressure and stay focused on their long-term trading plan.

Development of a Stress Management Plan:

Identification of Stress Sources:

The first step is to identify specific stress sources related to trading. These may include market volatility, financial losses, performance pressures, or unpredictable market conditions. Becoming aware of these stress factors allows for better understanding and the development of suitable strategies to manage them. Some points have already been mentioned in this book, but we wanted to consolidate them:

Establishment of Realistic Goals:

Setting realistic and achievable trading goals is crucial for stress reduction. Traders should focus on measurable and attainable goals, avoiding setting unrealistic expectations or seeking excessive short-term gains. With clear goals, traders can better manage pressure and remain focused on their long-term trading plan.

Development of Stress Management Techniques:

Once stress sources are identified, traders can begin to develop stress management techniques tailored to their individual needs. This may include strategies such as deep breathing, meditation, yoga, regular physical exercise, or guided visualization. The goal is to find activities that help calm the mind and reduce stress levels.

Creation of a Well-Being Routine:

Incorporating well-being practices into the daily routine is essential for maintaining mental and emotional balance. Traders can schedule dedicated times for relaxation, physical exercise, meditation, or other soothing activities throughout the day. A balanced routine can help reduce stress and promote a positive mindset.

Utilization of Emotion Management Techniques:

Learning to recognize and manage emotions is a crucial skill for reducing trading-related stress. Traders can use techniques such as emotion journaling, acceptance and mindfulness practice, and seeking a coach or mentor to help them develop effective strategies for managing the emotional ups and downs of trading.

Adaptability and Flexibility:

Finally, it is essential to be flexible and adaptable in stress management. Market conditions can change rapidly, and traders must be prepared to adjust their stress management plan accordingly. This may involve testing different techniques and seeing what works best in different trading situations.

Adopting a Long-Term Perspective:

Adopting a long-term perspective is crucial for traders seeking to effectively manage their stress and maintain their mental and emotional well-being. This approach involves stepping back from daily market fluctuations and focusing on longer-term goals. For trading enthusiasts, it can be tempting to get caught up in the rapid market movements and react excessively to price fluctuations.

However, this can lead to stress and anxiety as traders may constantly feel pressured to make impulsive decisions.

By adopting a long-term perspective, traders can reduce this stress by focusing on more fundamental factors and avoiding being distracted by short-term fluctuations. This allows them to make more thoughtful and informed decisions, considering the long-term evolution of the market rather than short-term movements.

Furthermore, a long-term perspective enables traders to better manage the emotional ups and downs that often accompany trading. Instead of reacting excessively to temporary losses or gains, traders can maintain a big picture view and stay focused on their longer-term goals.

Ultimately, adopting a long-term perspective allows trading enthusiasts to better manage their stress, make more informed decisions, and maintain a more stable and consistent approach to their trading practice. This not only contributes to their mental and emotional well-being but also to their long-term success in the financial markets.

Performance Anxiety Management:

Managing performance-related anxiety is a crucial aspect of trading, as it can significantly influence your decisions and financial results. As a passionate trader, you may find yourself facing different forms of anxiety, often triggered by various factors.

Fear of losing money is one of the main sources of anxiety for traders. This apprehension can be exacerbated by the pressure to generate consistent profits and outperform the market. You may feel constant tension when making trading decisions, fearing errors that could lead to significant financial losses.

Comparing yourself to other traders can also trigger anxiety. You may feel stressed and demoralized if you feel you are not performing as well as your peers. This social pressure can lead to irrational behavior and impulsive decisions in an attempt to compare favorably with others.

Additionally, lack of confidence in your skills and ability to make sound trading decisions can reinforce performance-related anxiety. Doubts and uncertainty can overwhelm you, compromising your ability to stay focused and follow your trading plan.

To effectively manage this anxiety, it is essential to implement stress and anxiety management strategies. This may include relaxation techniques such as deep breathing and meditation, as well as anxiety management methods like positive visualization and repetition of encouraging mantras.

Furthermore, establishing mental preparation routines before trading can help you feel more confident and calm. Success visualization exercises and mindfulness practices can help you stay present and focused during your trading sessions.

By taking a proactive approach to managing performance-related anxiety, you can improve your mental and emotional well-being, which will have a positive impact on your trading results.

Chapter 7: Case Studies and Practical Examples

7.1 Analysis of Real Trades with Explained Entries and Exits

Example 1: Trade on the EUR/USD Pair

In this example, I will delve into a detailed analysis of a trade on the EUR/USD currency pair, highlighting the various steps of my trading decision.

Context: The EUR/USD market exhibits a sustained bullish trend following favorable economic data from the Eurozone, including strong growth reports and encouraging economic indicators. The pair has recently surpassed key resistance levels and is currently in a consolidation phase near its recent highs.

Entry Point: After observing the persistent strength of the EUR/USD bullish trend, I decided to enter a long (buy) position as soon as the pair broke through the major resistance at 1.1500. This level was significant as it had repeatedly acted as a psychological barrier for traders and represented an important threshold to monitor.

Technical Analysis: Before making my decision, I conducted a thorough analysis of price charts, using a combination of Japanese candlesticks, trendlines, and technical indicators such as RSI and MACD. I also considered the broader market context, including economic and political developments that could influence the currency pair.

Trade Management: Once I entered the position, I immediately placed a stop-loss order just below the last significant low, which allowed me to limit losses in case of a sudden market reversal. I also set an initial profit target based on an analysis of potential short-term resistance levels.

Active Monitoring: After opening my position, I actively monitored the market's movement, adjusting my stop-loss and take-profit orders based on new developments. I also kept an eye on upcoming economic announcements and events that could impact the EUR/USD pair.

Exit Point: I took my profits when the pair reached the next resistance at 1.1650, which aligned with my predetermined profit target. By taking a disciplined approach and following my trading plan, I was able to secure a satisfactory gain while limiting my risks.

Conclusion: This trade on the EUR/USD illustrates the importance of thorough analysis, effective risk management, and rigorous discipline in price action trading.

By understanding the intricacies of the market and using proven strategies, traders can increase their chances of success and achieve their long-term trading goals.

Example 2: Trading on a Breakout of Support Level on the EUR/USD

Context: The foreign exchange market is characterized by high volatility due to significant economic announcements, including monetary policy decisions from the Federal Reserve and the European Central Bank. The EUR/USD is one of the most popular currency pairs and is responsive to economic events.

Entry Point: After observing prolonged consolidation around a major support level at 1.1700, I decided to enter a long position on the EUR/USD following a convincing bullish breakout above this key level. The breakout was confirmed by an increase in trading volume, indicating a renewed interest from buyers.

Technical Analysis: I used a combination of technical indicators such as exponential moving averages and MACD to confirm my entry decision. Additionally, I monitored Fibonacci levels to identify potential future resistance zones to take profits.

Trade Management: Once in position, I placed a stop-loss order just below the recently broken support level to limit losses in case of a market reversal. I also set an initial profit target based on an attractive risk/reward ratio, aiming for a resistance zone near 1.1900.

Active Monitoring: I closely followed the movement of the EUR/USD market, adjusting my orders based on new information and movements in other major currency pairs. I also took into account upcoming economic announcements, such as inflation figures and interest rate decisions, which could influence the market's direction.

Exit Point: I decided to exit my position when the EUR/USD reached the anticipated resistance zone near 1.1900, where I took partial profits. I also moved my stop-loss order to a breakeven level to protect my remaining gains in case of a market reversal.

Conclusion: This trade on the EUR/USD illustrates the importance of identifying key support and resistance levels and using breakouts of these levels to identify potential trading opportunities. By adopting a disciplined approach and using solid technical analysis, traders can capitalize on directional movements in the foreign exchange market and achieve their trading goals.

Example 3: Loss Management on a False Breakout of Resistance Level on the USD/JPY

Context: The currency market is subject to unpredictable movements, and even with careful analysis, it is possible to incur losses. This example illustrates the management of a loss on a false breakout of a major resistance level on the USD/JPY pair.

Entry Point: After observing a sharp rise in the USD/JPY and an apparent breakout of a key resistance level at 110.50, I decided to enter a long position, anticipating a continuation of the bullish trend. The breakout seemed to be supported by bullish momentum and an increase in trading volume.

Technical Analysis: I used technical indicators such as RSI and MACD to confirm my entry decision, which seemed promising given the favorable economic conditions in the United States. However, I failed to take into account signs of divergence and overbought conditions on these indicators.

Trade Management: Unfortunately, shortly after opening my long position, the market reversed direction and rejected the breakout of the resistance level. Faced with this situation, I quickly reacted by placing a tight stop-loss order just below the initial entry point to limit losses in case of a sudden market reversal.

Active Monitoring: I closely monitored the movement of the USD/JPY market and reevaluated my position based on new developments. Although my initial analysis indicated a favorable trading opportunity, I quickly recognized the invalidation of this perspective and acted accordingly to minimize losses.

Exit Point: When the USD/JPY continued to decline and breached my stop-loss level, I accepted the loss and closed my position in accordance with my risk management strategy. Although this resulted in a financial loss, I recognized the importance of adhering to my trading rules and preserving my capital to continue trading.

Conclusion: This example demonstrates the importance of risk management and responsiveness to rapid changes in financial markets. Even with solid technical analysis, it is possible to incur losses, but by applying rigorous discipline and actively managing positions, traders can mitigate losses and maintain a long-term perspective in their trading approach.

7.2 Reflections on the Decisions Made and the Results Obtained

In this section, we delve into a critical introspection of the decisions made during our trades and the resulting outcomes. This reflective process is crucial for assessing our performance, identifying our strengths and weaknesses, and enhancing our trading approach.

As traders, it's vital to step back after each transaction, whether it's a success or failure, to grasp the reasons behind our actions and their impact on our results. This retrospective analysis can aid in better understanding our behaviors and thinking patterns, subsequently informing our future decisions.

When reflecting on our decisions, we should ponder over a few key questions:

> Initial Objective: What was my goal in initiating this position? Was it realistic and clearly defined?

> Preceding Analysis: Did I conduct a thorough market analysis before making my decision? Did I consider all relevant factors?

> Risk Management: Did I implement adequate risk management measures, such as stop-loss and take-profit orders? Did I adhere to my risk management rules?

> Emotion and Discipline: Did I allow my emotions to influence my trading decisions? Did I adhere to my trading strategy and maintain discipline, even when things didn't go as planned?

> Continuous Learning: What did I learn from this experience? What are the lessons I can extract to enhance myself as a trader in the future?

By honestly addressing these questions and critically analyzing our decisions and outcomes, we can progress as traders. This enables us to pinpoint what works well and what can be improved, leading to a more effective and consistent approach to price action-based trading.

Ultimately, reflecting on our decisions and results is a vital component of our development as traders. It helps us become more aware of our behaviors and trading habits, which can lead to continual improvement in our performance in the financial markets.

Chapter 8: Advanced Price Action Trading Techniques

8.1 Utilizing Market Correlation to Enhance Trading Signals

Identifying Correlations:

Begin by identifying correlations between different financial assets, such as currencies, stocks, commodities, and indices. Correlations can be positive, negative, or neutral, and they can vary based on market conditions and economic events.

Analyzing Correlation Factors:

Examine the factors influencing correlations between markets, such as central bank monetary policies, key economic indicators, geopolitical movements, and global macroeconomic conditions. Understanding these factors can help anticipate changes in correlation and adjust strategies accordingly.

Using Correlations as Confirmation Indicators:

Market correlations can serve as confirmation indicators for trading signals. For instance, if two assets are strongly correlated and one shows a clear buying signal, it can strengthen the validity of the signal for the other asset.

Risk Diversification:

Market correlations can also be used to diversify risk in a trading portfolio. By selecting assets with low or negative correlations, traders can reduce exposure to specific market risk and protect their capital against unforeseen fluctuations.

Risk Management:

As with any trading strategy, risk management remains crucial when utilizing market correlation. It's important to diversify positions and not overexpose the portfolio to a single correlation. Additionally, traders should always use stop-loss orders to limit losses in case of unexpected market movements.

In conclusion, utilizing market correlation can be a powerful tool to enhance trading signals and identify lucrative opportunities. However, it requires a deep understanding of the relationships between different markets and careful risk management.

8.2 Short-Term Trading vs. Long-Term Trading: Strategy Comparison

Short-Term Trading:

Short-term trading involves opening and closing positions within a relatively short timeframe, ranging from minutes to days. Short-term traders often seek short-term price movements and exploit market volatility to make quick profits.

Advantages:
Frequent Opportunities:

Short-term trading offers numerous opportunities to profit as traders can capitalize on daily price fluctuations in financial markets.

High Liquidity:

Assets traded in the short term, such as major currency pairs or highly liquid stocks, provide high liquidity, allowing traders to enter and exit positions easily.

Less Risk of Reversal:

Short-term traders are less exposed to risks associated with long-term macroeconomic events since their positions are typically short-lived.

Disadvantages:
Transaction Costs:

Short-term trading can be costly due to more frequent transaction fees, such as brokerage commissions and bid-ask spreads.

High Stress:

The fast-paced nature of short-term trading can lead to high stress as traders need to constantly monitor markets and make quick decisions.

Market Noise Sensitivity:

Short-term traders are often more sensitive to market noise, such as rumors and economic announcements, which can result in increased volatility and erratic price movements.

Long-Term Trading:

Long-term trading involves holding positions for weeks, months, or even years, with the hope of achieving significant long-term gains. Long-term traders adopt a more patient approach and look for sustainable trends in the markets.

Advantages:

Less Stress:

Long-term traders experience less daily trading stress as they don't need to constantly monitor markets and can make more thoughtful decisions.

Reduced Transaction Costs:

Since long-term traders execute fewer trades, they can reduce their overall transaction costs, which can be a long-term financial advantage.

Exploitation of Major Trends:

Long-term trading allows traders to capitalize on major trends in the markets, which can lead to significant gains when these trends materialize.

Disadvantages:
Fewer Opportunities:

Long-term trading offers fewer trading opportunities compared to short-term trading as long-term price movements are less frequent.

Exposure to Macroeconomic Risks:

Long-term traders are more exposed to risks associated with long-term macroeconomic events, such as political changes and economic fluctuations.

Tendency to Hold Losses:

Long-term traders may tend to hold losses longer in the hope that the market will turn in their favor, which can result in significant losses if the trend persists.

In conclusion, the choice between short-term trading and long-term trading depends on the trader's personal preferences, lifestyle, risk tolerance, and financial goals. There is no right or wrong approach, but it is essential for each trader to understand the characteristics and requirements of each trading style before making investment decisions.

Chapter 9: Price Action Based Automated Trading

9.1 Introduction to Automated Trading Systems

The introduction of automated trading systems marks a significant evolution in the world of price action-based trading. These systems, also known as trading robots or algorithms, use computer algorithms to execute transactions in financial markets without direct human intervention.

This automation offers many advantages to traders but also presents unique challenges to consider.

Advantages of Automated Trading Systems:

Fast and Precise Execution: Automated systems can execute orders instantly and accurately, enabling traders to quickly seize trading opportunities and minimize delays due to market fluctuations.

Elimination of Emotional Bias: By eliminating the emotional aspect of the decision-making process, automated systems can help avoid common human errors such as impulsive trading or sentiment-based decisions.

Ability to Manage Multiple Markets and Instruments: Trading robots can monitor and trade on multiple markets and instruments simultaneously, allowing traders to explore a wide range of trading opportunities without being limited by their own capacity to follow the markets.

Facilitated Backtesting and Optimization: Automated systems enable traders to backtest and optimize their strategies efficiently, using historical data to evaluate past performance and adjust system parameters.

24/7 Trading Capability: Through automation, traders can monitor and trade in the markets 24/7, enabling them to seize opportunities even outside traditional trading hours.

However, automated trading also presents challenges:

Dependency on Technology: Automated systems rely on the reliability of technology and may be vulnerable to computer failures, internet outages, or programming errors.

Risk of Over-Optimization: It is possible to over-optimize an automated system by excessively adjusting its parameters to match historical data, which can lead to disappointing performance in real market conditions.

Need for Continuous Monitoring: Although automated systems can operate autonomously, they require continuous monitoring to ensure they are performing as expected and to intervene if necessary.

Complexity of Dynamic Markets: Financial markets are dynamic and unpredictable, making it difficult for automated systems to quickly adapt to unexpected changes or events.

Automating price action-based trading provides traders with the opportunity to enhance the efficiency, speed, and precision of their operations.

However, it is important to understand the advantages and challenges associated with this approach and to remain vigilant in monitoring and managing automated systems to ensure optimal results in financial markets.

9.2 Development of Algorithmic Trading Strategies

In this section, we delve into the fascinating world of developing algorithmic trading strategies. Algorithmic trading strategies, often referred to as "automated trading" or "algorithmic trading," are computer programs designed to automatically execute buy or sell operations in financial markets based on predefined rules.

Strategy Design:

The first step in developing an algorithmic strategy is design. Traders must clearly define the objectives of their strategy, whether it's to generate consistent profits, reduce losses, or take advantage of specific market conditions. Next, they identify key parameters to integrate into the program, such as technical indicators, price patterns, or fundamental events, which will serve as the basis for automated decision-making.

Programming and Testing:
Once the design is established, traders move on to the programming phase. They translate their trading rules into computer code, often using programming languages like Python, C++, or MQL4/5. During this phase, it's essential to consider aspects such as data management, market connectivity, and system security.

Once the program is written, traders conduct rigorous testing to evaluate its performance. This often involves using historical data to simulate the program's behavior in real market conditions. These tests help identify the strengths and weaknesses of the strategy and make necessary adjustments.

Optimization and Validation:

After initial testing, traders proceed to optimize the strategy. This may include parameter adjustments, exploring new ideas, or incorporating advanced machine learning techniques to improve performance. Once optimization is complete, the strategy undergoes additional validation to confirm its robustness in various market conditions.

Real-Time Implementation:

Once the strategy is developed, tested, and validated, it's ready to be implemented in real-time on financial markets. Traders must choose an appropriate trading platform and ensure their system is capable of operating reliably and securely in a live trading environment.

Monitoring and Maintenance:

Finally, once the strategy is operational, traders must carefully monitor its performance and make adjustments as necessary. This may include code updates, parameter changes, or adaptations to new market conditions. Continuous monitoring is essential to ensure the strategy remains effective and responsive to market developments.

In summary, the development of algorithmic trading strategies is a complex but potentially lucrative process for traders. By combining a deep understanding of financial markets with programming and data analysis skills, traders can create automated systems that effectively exploit trading opportunities and minimize risks.

9.3: Backtesting and Optimization of Automated Strategies

Backtesting, or historical testing, is a crucial step in the development of algorithmic trading strategies. It involves evaluating the performance of a strategy using historical data to simulate its behavior in past market conditions.

Here are the key aspects of backtesting and optimizing automated strategies:

Data Collection and Preparation:

The first step in the backtesting process is collecting and preparing the necessary historical data. This includes price data such as open, close, high, and low prices, as well as other relevant data like trading volume. High-quality and well-cleaned data are essential for accurate results.

Definition of Trading Rules:

Once the data is prepared, traders define the trading rules to be tested. This includes technical indicators, entry and exit conditions, risk management criteria, etc. The rules must be clearly defined and unambiguous to ensure reliable results during backtesting.

Execution of Backtesting:

After defining the trading rules, backtesting is executed by applying these rules to historical data to simulate transactions. The strategy's performance is measured based on various indicators such as returns, drawdown, Sharpe ratio, etc. Traders can then evaluate the strategy's effectiveness in different market conditions.

Analysis of Results:

Once backtesting is complete, the results are analyzed in detail to identify the strengths and weaknesses of the strategy. Traders examine overall returns, periods of gain and loss, risk/return ratios, and other relevant metrics. This helps determine if the strategy is viable and worthy of further pursuit.

Strategy Optimization:

Based on the results of backtesting, traders may optimize their strategy by making adjustments to parameters or trading rules. This may involve modifications to improve performance, reduce risks, or adapt to new market conditions. Optimization is an iterative process aimed at maximizing returns while minimizing potential losses.

Validation and Market Condition Sensitivity:

It's essential to validate backtesting results by comparing them with real-time data and testing the strategy in various market conditions. Traders must also assess the strategy's sensitivity to market changes and ensure it remains robust in different environments.

In conclusion, backtesting and optimization of automated strategies are essential steps to ensure the reliability and profitability of algorithmic trading systems.

9.4: Implementation and Monitoring of Automated Trading Systems

Once an automated trading strategy has been developed, backtested, and optimized, the next crucial step is its implementation and monitoring on real-time markets. Here are the key aspects of implementing and monitoring automated trading systems:

Choice of Trading Platform:

The first decision to make is choosing the trading platform on which the automated system will be executed. There are many options available, each with its own features and capabilities. Traders must select a reliable, secure platform compatible with their trading strategy.

System Configuration:

After selecting the trading platform, the automated system needs to be configured according to the trading rules defined during the development stage. This includes programming indicators, entry and exit conditions, risk management parameters, etc. Configuration must be done accurately to ensure the system operates correctly.

Real-world Testing:

Before deploying the system on real funds, it's advisable to test it in a simulated trading environment or using recent historical data to verify its functionality. This helps detect any potential issues or programming errors before they affect live system performance.

Continuous Monitoring:

Once the system is in place, it's essential to monitor it closely to ensure it operates as expected. Traders should monitor signals generated by the system, performance of executed trades, and other relevant indicators. This allows for quickly identifying potential issues and making adjustments if necessary.

Adaptation to Market Conditions:

Market conditions are constantly changing, and automated systems must be able to adapt to these changes. Traders need to monitor the system's performance in different market contexts and be ready to make adjustments or modifications to maintain its profitability.

Performance Analysis:

Traders must regularly review the performance of their automated system by analyzing past trade results. This involves monitoring key indicators such as total returns, success rate, risk/return ratio, maximum drawdown, etc. Performance analysis helps evaluate the system's effectiveness and identify areas for improvement.

Weakness Identification:

By examining losing trades or periods of underperformance, traders can identify potential weaknesses in their automated system. This may include issues such as inappropriate parameters, unfavorable market conditions, or programming errors. Identifying these weaknesses is crucial for making adjustments and improving system performance in the future.

Continuous Optimization:

Based on performance analysis conclusions, traders need to make continuous adjustments and optimizations to their automated system. This may involve modifying trading parameters, adding filters or additional rules, or even completely redesigning the system if necessary. The goal is to constantly optimize the system to adapt to changing market conditions and maximize profitability.

Use of External Data:

In addition to internal data generated by the automated trading system, traders can also leverage external data to improve performance. This may include using economic data, sector reports, financial news, or even data from other trading systems. Incorporating this external data can provide additional insights and help refine automated trading strategies.

Risk Management:

Risk management remains a top priority when using automated trading systems. Traders must set clear risk limits, such as stop-loss and take-profit levels, and ensure the system adheres to these limits at all times. They must also closely monitor position size and correlation with other strategies or positions in their overall portfolio.

Implementing and monitoring automated trading systems require careful planning, precise configuration, and continuous monitoring.

Chapter 10: Evolution and Adaptation in a Changing Market Environment

10.1 Importance of Adaptability in Trading

In the realm of trading, adaptability stands as a crucial skill enabling traders to thrive in an ever-evolving market environment. The significance of adaptability lies in the ability to swiftly adjust to market condition changes, new information, and unforeseen events. In this chapter, we'll delve into why adaptability is vital in trading and how traders can cultivate this trait to enhance their success in financial markets.

Why Adaptability is Crucial in Trading:
Market Volatility:

Financial markets are inherently volatile, subject to rapid and unpredictable fluctuations. Traders must swiftly adapt to price changes and market conditions to seize trading opportunities and avoid potential losses.

Economic Changes:

Global economic events such as interest rate announcements, economic reports, and political developments can significantly impact financial markets. Traders must swiftly analyze these events and adjust their strategies accordingly to capitalize on opportunities or hedge against risks.

Uncertainty:

Uncertainty is an inherent characteristic of financial markets, and traders must be prepared to navigate uncertainty and make decisions in conditions of imperfect information. Being adaptable allows them to remain flexible and adjust to changes in market sentiment.

Technology and Innovation:

The rapid advancement of technology and innovation in trading can also lead to swift changes in trading methods and available tools. Traders must be open to new technologies and ready to integrate them into their trading strategies to remain competitive in the market.

How to Develop Adaptability in Trading:
Continuing Education:

Traders must engage in continuous education to stay informed about the latest market trends, economic developments, and technological advancements. This enables them to develop a thorough understanding of the markets and adapt their strategies accordingly.

Mental Flexibility:

Being mentally flexible is essential for adapting to changes in market conditions and new information. Traders must be willing to question their assumptions, adjust their perspectives, and change course if necessary.

Risk Management:

Prudent risk management is a key element of adaptability in trading. Traders must be willing to reduce their risk exposure in unfavorable market conditions and protect their capital against potential losses.

Reflective Analysis:

Traders must regularly reflect on their past performance, successes, and failures, and draw lessons from their experiences. This allows them to identify areas for improvement and adjust their strategies accordingly.

By developing their adaptability, traders can navigate better in an ever-changing market environment and enhance their ability to make informed and timely decisions in financial markets.

10.2 Continuous Review and Adjustment of Trading Strategies

In trading, continuous review and adjustment of strategies are essential to remain competitive and successful in financial markets. Market conditions are constantly evolving, and traders must be ready to adapt their approaches accordingly to maintain their competitive edge. In this section, we'll delve into the importance of continuous review and adjustment of trading strategies, along with best practices to achieve it.

Importance of Continuous Review and Adjustment:
Adaptation to Market Conditions:

Financial markets are dynamic and subject to constant changes. What worked yesterday may not work today due to new trends, economic factors, or volatility.

Continuous review of strategies allows traders to adapt quickly to these changes and capitalize on new opportunities.

Performance Optimization:

By regularly reviewing their trading strategies, traders can identify aspects of their approach that are performing well and those that could be improved. This enables them to optimize their performance by leveraging their strengths and mitigating their weaknesses.

Risk Management:

Continuous review of trading strategies also allows traders to better manage risk. By identifying areas where risk is too high or poorly managed, traders can adjust their strategies to reduce potential losses and protect their capital.

Anticipation of Changes:

By staying constantly vigilant of changes in financial markets, traders can anticipate emerging trends and adjust their strategies accordingly. This gives them a competitive advantage by enabling them to make informed decisions before trends become evident to everyone.

Best Practices for Continuous Review and Adjustment:
Performance Analysis:

Traders must regularly analyze their past performance to identify trends, patterns, and areas for improvement. This can be done using trading journals, analysis reports, and performance evaluation software.

Market Conditions Monitoring:

Continuous monitoring of market conditions is essential to detect potential changes and adjust strategies accordingly. Traders must be attentive to economic news, political events, and price movements in financial markets.

Testing and Validation:

Before implementing major adjustments, traders should test and validate their new strategies in simulated or historical market conditions. This allows them to measure the effectiveness of proposed adjustments before applying them in a real environment.

Mental Flexibility:

Traders must be willing to challenge their own beliefs and adjust their strategies based on new information and changes in market conditions. This requires some mental flexibility and openness to experimentation.

By continuously reviewing and adjusting their trading strategies, traders can stay in tune with ever-evolving financial markets and improve their long-term success prospects.

10.3 Strategies for Dealing with Unexpected Events in the Markets

In the world of trading, dealing with unexpected events in the markets is a crucial skill for any serious trader. Financial markets are often subject to unforeseen events such as economic announcements, sudden political developments, or geopolitical crises, which can lead to increased volatility and rapid price movements. In this section, we will explore effective strategies for coping with these unexpected events and successfully navigating through them.

Strategies for Dealing with Unexpected Events:

Maintain Calm and Discipline: When unexpected events occur in the markets, it is essential to remain calm and disciplined. Reacting emotionally can lead to impulsive and irrational decisions that may worsen the situation. Keep your trading objectives in mind and stick to your pre-established trading plan.

Risk Management: Risk management is of paramount importance when dealing with unexpected events. Use stop-loss orders to limit potential losses and protect your capital. Also, ensure to diversify your portfolio to reduce the impact of a specific event on a single position.

Continuous Monitoring: Stay constantly vigilant of news and developments in the markets. Use reliable and up-to-date sources of information to stay informed about events that could impact your positions. Be prepared to react quickly if necessary.

Assessment of Impact: Evaluate the potential impact of the event on your positions and your portfolio as a whole. Determine whether the event is likely to have a short-term or long-term effect on the markets, and adjust your positions accordingly.

Adjustment of Strategy: If necessary, adjust your trading strategy to accommodate the new market situation. This may involve taking defensive positions, reducing risk exposure, or seeking out new trading opportunities that may arise from the event.

Learning and Adaptation: Use every unexpected event as an opportunity for learning and improvement. Analyze your decisions and their outcomes, identify lessons learned, and use them to refine your approach in the future.

Communication with Other Traders: Engage with other traders to share ideas, perspectives, and strategies for dealing with unexpected events. Collaborating with other traders can provide valuable support and advice in times of market turbulence.

Ultimately, the ability to deal with unexpected events in the markets relies on preparation, discipline, and the ability to remain agile and adaptable in the face of uncertainty.

10.4 Long-Term Planning for Trading Sustainability

In the world of trading, long-term planning is essential to ensure sustainability and continued success in price action-based trading. This section will focus on the importance of long-term strategic planning and key elements to consider for long-term trading sustainability.

Long-Term Planning for Trading Sustainability:

Establishment of Clear and Realistic Goals: It all starts with setting clear and realistic goals. Define your long-term trading goals considering your financial aspirations, risk tolerance, and trading skills. These goals should be Specific, Measurable, Achievable, Relevant, and Time-bound (SMART).

Development of a Solid Strategy: Build a robust and well-thought-out trading strategy that aligns with your long-term goals. Your strategy should include clear rules for entry and exit positions, effective risk management techniques, and criteria for performance evaluation.

Example of a Solid Strategy:

Objective: Maximize profits by identifying and capturing short-term price movements in the forex market.

Approach:

Technical Analysis: Utilize in-depth analysis of price charts, focusing on candlestick patterns, support and resistance levels, as well as technical indicators such as moving averages and Bollinger Bands.

Trend Identification: Search for short-term trends by analyzing price patterns and identifying key levels where prices have historically bounced or broken.

Risk Management: Use stop-loss orders to limit losses in case of unfavorable price movements, with prudent management of position size to limit exposure to risk.

Trade Management: Set clear profit targets based on a favorable risk/reward ratio. Use dynamic stop-losses to lock in profits when the market moves in our favor.

Continuous Monitoring: Continuously monitor open positions to detect signs of trend reversal or market consolidation. Adjust stop-loss orders and profit targets based on market conditions.

Performance Evaluation: Regularly analyze trading results to assess the effectiveness of the strategy. Identify strengths and weaknesses to make adjustments and improve overall performance.

Portfolio Diversification: Portfolio diversification is crucial to reduce risk and enhance long-term trading sustainability. Allocate your capital across different markets, financial instruments, and trading strategies to avoid over-reliance on a single asset or income source.

Prudent Risk Management: Adopt a cautious approach to risk management by using stop-loss orders, appropriate position sizes, and judicious capital allocation. Limit your exposure to risk on each trade and ensure not to risk more than what you can afford to lose.

Continuous Learning and Development: Invest in your professional development by pursuing continuous education and honing your trading skills. Stay updated on the latest market trends, advanced trading techniques, and technological innovations in algorithmic trading.

Adaptability and Flexibility: Maintain adaptability and flexibility in response to changes in the financial markets. Market conditions are constantly evolving, and the ability to adapt quickly to new situations is essential for sustaining long-term trading success.

Regular Performance Evaluation: Conduct regular evaluations of your trading performance to identify strengths and weaknesses in your approach. Analyze your trades, identify recurring errors, and make necessary adjustments to your strategy to improve long-term results.

Emotional Management: Learn to manage your emotions and maintain a disciplined, goal-oriented mindset. Avoid impulsive and emotional decisions that can jeopardize your long-term results and stay focused on your trading plan.

In conclusion, long-term planning is the key to sustainability in price action-based trading. By establishing clear goals, developing a solid strategy, effectively managing risk, and remaining adaptable to market changes, traders can enhance their chances of success and maintain a sustainable career in trading.

Chapter 11: Continuous Education and Resources for Traders

11.1 Importance of Ongoing Learning in Trading

In your journey as a trader, whether you're a beginner or experienced, it's crucial to recognize the importance of continuous learning. Financial markets are dynamic and constantly evolving, and to stay at the top of your game, you must invest in your education continuously.

Why Continuous Learning is Crucial:

Market Evolution: Markets are influenced by a multitude of factors that are constantly changing. By staying informed about the latest trends and developments, you can adjust your trading strategy accordingly and make more informed decisions.

Adapting to New Technologies: Technological advancements are rapidly transforming the trading landscape. By staying up-to-date with the latest technologies and learning how to use them effectively, you can gain a competitive edge in the market.

Skill Enhancement: Trading is a skill that improves with practice and continuous study. By investing in your personal development, you can refine your skills in technical analysis, risk management, and trading psychology, which can lead to better long-term results.

Risk Reduction: A deep understanding of the markets and solid trading skills can help you reduce your exposure to risk and avoid potential market pitfalls. By continuously learning, you can make more informed decisions and better protect your capital.

Strategies for Effective Continuous Learning:

Reading: Explore a variety of resources, from books to online articles, to deepen your understanding of trading. Choose works written by industry experts to gain valuable insights and practical advice.

Online Training: Online courses and webinars offer flexibility to learn at your own pace. Look for training programs delivered by trusted professionals and make sure to stay updated with the latest market trends.

Practice: Nothing beats hands-on experience. Use demo accounts to test new strategies without risking real capital, then move on to real accounts with modest amounts to put your knowledge into practice.

Networking: Join online trading communities, forums, and discussion groups to exchange ideas and experiences with other traders. Knowledge sharing can help broaden your perspective and discover new trading opportunities.

In conclusion, continuous learning is essential for success in trading. By investing in your education and staying constantly informed, you can improve your skills, reduce your risks, and remain competitive in an ever-changing market environment.

11.2 Sources of Information and Education for Traders

For traders eager to learn, there are numerous accessible sources of information and education. Whether you're a beginner or experienced, finding the right resources can make all the difference in your trading journey. Here are some of the best sources you can access:

Specialized Books: Books written by industry experts offer a wealth of valuable information on various aspects of trading, from technical analysis to market psychology.

Online Courses: Online learning platforms offer a variety of trading courses, ranging from basics to advanced techniques. Look for courses taught by industry professionals and check student reviews to find the programs that best suit your needs.

Webinars and Seminars: Many brokers and trading experts regularly host free or paid online webinars and seminars. These events allow you to learn proven trading strategies and ask questions directly to the presenters.

Trading Forums: Online forums provide spaces to discuss the latest market trends, share trading ideas, and ask questions to the community. Joining these forums can help you expand your network and benefit from the knowledge of other traders.

YouTube Channels and Podcasts: Many traders and experts share their knowledge and tips via YouTube videos and podcasts. Subscribe to quality channels and relevant podcasts to stay informed about the latest market trends and best trading practices.

Mentorship: Working with an experienced mentor can accelerate your learning and provide personalized guidance to improve your trading skills. Look for mentors who have successful experience in financial markets and are willing to share their knowledge.

By exploring these different sources of information and education, you can enrich your understanding of trading and develop the skills needed to succeed in financial markets. Don't be afraid to explore and diversify your learning sources to gain a broader and deeper perspective.

11.3 Trading Communities and Support Networks for Traders

In the trading world, being part of an active community can be extremely beneficial for your development as a trader. Trading communities provide an environment where you can share ideas, get advice, and benefit from the support of like-minded peers. Here are some reasons why you should consider joining a trading community:

Exchange of Ideas and Strategies: Trading communities are places where traders can discuss the latest market trends, share their analyses, and exchange trading ideas. Participating in these discussions can help you discover new strategies and improve your own approach to trading.

Support and Encouragement: Trading can sometimes be lonely and stressful. Being part of a community gives you access to a support network where you can share your successes, challenges, and frustrations with other traders who understand what you're going through. Receiving encouragement and advice can help you stay motivated and overcome obstacles.

Continuous Learning: By interacting with other traders, you can continue to learn and grow. Community members can share educational resources, recommend books or courses, and keep you informed about the latest news and important events in financial markets.

Collaboration Opportunities: Trading communities can also offer collaboration and partnership opportunities. You can find people with similar interests and goals with whom you can work together to develop trading strategies or explore new markets.

Accountability: By being part of a community, you commit to being accountable for your actions to your peers. Knowing that you are accountable to other traders can help you stay disciplined and stick to your trading plan.

Finding the right trading community can make a huge difference in your trading journey. Look for online or local communities that align with your interests and trading style, and don't hesitate to actively get involved to make the most out of it.

11.4 Investment in Professional Development Programs

Investing in professional development programs can be a crucial step in improving your trading skills and enhancing your success in financial markets. Here are some reasons why you should consider dedicating time and resources to your professional development:

Specialized Knowledge Acquisition: Professional development programs are designed to provide thorough and specialized training in various aspects of trading. Whether you're a novice or an experienced trader, these programs can help you acquire new skills, deepen your understanding of the markets, and stay updated on the latest trends and technologies.

Access to Experts and Mentors: The best professional development programs are led by industry experts who have practical trading experience. By participating in these programs, you have the opportunity to learn directly from the best, ask questions, and benefit from the guidance of experienced mentors.

Networking Opportunities: Professional development programs often provide opportunities to meet other like-minded traders and build relationships with industry professionals. These networks can be valuable for exchanging ideas, finding potential trading partners, and staying connected to the broader trading community.

Enhancement of Discipline and Consistency: Following a professional development program requires commitment, discipline, and consistency. By investing time and effort in your education, you reinforce these essential qualities for success in trading. You also learn to follow a structured plan and maintain a methodical approach in your trading.

Acceleration of Learning Curve: Professional development programs are designed to provide targeted and organized educational content, which can help you progress more quickly in your trading learning journey. Instead of trying to navigate alone through a sea of scattered information, you benefit from a structured and guided framework to develop your skills.

Investment in Your Future: Ultimately, investing in professional development programs is an investment in your own future as a trader. The knowledge and skills you gain through these programs can have a lasting impact on your trading performance and long-term success.

Choosing the right professional development programs is crucial. Look for reputable programs led by credible experts and offering content relevant to your specific trading goals. By investing in your professional development, you are taking concrete steps to improve your trading skills and achieve your financial objectives.

Conclusion

In this conclusion, I aim to provide you with a summary of the key points covered in this book, along with encouragement and advice to support you on your trading journey. Finally, I'd like to express my gratitude to you, dear readers, and share some perspectives for the future.

Throughout these pages, we have delved deeply into the fundamentals of price action trading. We have covered various topics, from technical analysis to trading psychology, advanced trading techniques, and strategy automation. You have learned to interpret price movements, manage your emotions, identify trading opportunities, and much more.

As a trading enthusiast, I encourage you to continue your quest for knowledge and experience. Stay curious, develop a solid trading discipline, learn to manage your emotions, and be ready to adapt to market changes. Don't hesitate to surround yourself with mentors and join trading communities to share your ideas and experiences.

I sincerely thank you for reading this book and investing in your development as a trader. Your commitment and passion are key to your future success. As you continue your journey in the world of trading, always remember that every experience is an opportunity for learning and growth.

For the future, I encourage you to remain ambitious, realistic about risks, determined, and persistent. The financial markets are vast and full of opportunities for those who are willing to seize them. Keep exploring, learning, and evolving as a trader.

Thank you again for your trust and commitment. I wish you every possible success on your trading journey.

Glossary

Versatility of PA Trading: The ability of price action trading to be applied across different financial markets and timeframes.

Market Psychology: The study of market participants' behavior and its impact on price movements.

Japanese Candlesticks: A charting technique displaying open, close, high, and low levels for each time period.

False Signals: Incorrect or misleading trading signals generated by price movement analysis.

Continuous Learning and Practice: The necessity for traders to acquire knowledge and develop skills through regular study and trading practice.

Bullish/Bearish Trend: The general direction of prices on a chart, indicating an increase (bullish) or decrease (bearish) in prices over time.

Hammer: A Japanese candlestick pattern indicating potential bullish reversal after a period of decline, characterized by a small lower wick and a body near the highs.

Support and Resistance Levels: Levels on a chart where prices have historically bounced or stalled, often considered as trading opportunity zones.

Evening Star: A Japanese candlestick pattern formed by a large bullish candle followed by a small bearish candle, indicating potential bearish reversal.

Fibonacci Retracements: Potential support and resistance levels based on the Fibonacci sequence, often used by traders to identify entry and exit points in financial markets.

Pivot Points: Support and resistance levels calculated from previous prices, used by traders to anticipate future price movements and set profit and loss targets.

Breakout: A price movement that exceeds a key support or resistance level, indicating a potential change in market direction.

Stop-Loss: A trading order designed to limit losses by automatically closing a position when the price reaches a predetermined level.

Profit Target: A predefined price level where a trader plans to take profits by closing a winning position.

Oscillators: Technical indicators used to identify overbought or oversold conditions in a financial market, providing potential reversal signals.

Trend Reversal: A trend reversal occurs when the price direction changes, transitioning from a bullish trend to a bearish trend, or vice versa. Traders seek to identify these reversals to profit from new price movements.

Divergence: Divergence occurs when there is a discrepancy between price movements and technical indicators, such as RSI or MACD. This can signal a weakening of the current trend and a possible imminent reversal.

Candlestick Patterns: Candlestick patterns are specific configurations of candles on a price chart that provide indications of future price movements. For example, a shooting star or inverted hammer may signal a potential trend reversal.

Fibonacci Levels: Fibonacci retracement levels are areas on a price chart calculated using Fibonacci ratios. These levels are often used by traders to identify support and resistance zones and anticipate trend reversals.

Signal Confirmation: Confirmation of trend reversal signals is essential to validate traders' forecasts. This may involve the use of additional technical indicators or confirmation by other market elements.

Trend Continuation: Trend continuation occurs when the current price direction persists. Traders seek to identify these opportunities to enter positions that follow the dominant trend.

Moving Averages: Moving averages are technical analysis tools that smooth price data to identify the general direction of a trend. They are often used to confirm the current trend.

Momentum Indicators: Momentum indicators, such as RSI or MACD, measure the strength of a current trend. High readings indicate a strong trend that could continue.

Volatility: Volatility measures the variation in prices of a financial asset over a given period. High volatility indicates significant price fluctuations, while low volatility indicates more modest fluctuations.

Trailing Stop-Loss: A trailing stop-loss is a type of stop-loss order that automatically follows price movement.

Frequently Asked Questions:

How can price action trading be profitable for traders?
- Answer: Price action trading allows traders to make decisions based on actual price movements in the market, rather than relying solely on technical indicators. By directly analyzing past and current price movements, traders can identify significant chart patterns and emerging trends, enabling them to make informed decisions on their positions.

What are the advantages of using Japanese candlesticks in price action trading?
- Answer: Japanese candlesticks provide a visual representation of price movements, offering traders a deeper understanding of market psychology. Different candlestick patterns, such as the hammer or shooting star, provide insights into potential trend reversals or continuations, helping traders make informed decisions.

Why is risk management crucial for the success of price action trading?
- Answer: Risk management is essential as it allows traders to control their losses and protect their capital. By using stop-loss orders and proper position sizing techniques, traders can limit their losses in case of unfavorable price movements, which is crucial for maintaining long-term sustainability and profitability in trading.

How can traders effectively identify support and resistance levels?
- Answer: Support and resistance levels are often identified by examining past price charts and spotting areas where prices have historically bounced or stalled. Traders can also use tools such as trendlines, Fibonacci retracements, and pivot points to confirm these levels and incorporate them into their trading decisions.

What are the main challenges traders face when using price action trading?
- Answer: Some of the main challenges include the need to remain disciplined and control emotions, the ability to accurately interpret candlestick patterns and chart configurations, as well as effectively managing risk to avoid significant losses.

Why is adaptability important for traders using price action trading?
- Answer: Adaptability is crucial because market conditions are constantly changing. Traders must be able to quickly adjust to these changes by modifying their strategies or making different decisions based on new information available.

What are the best practices for maximizing profits while minimizing risks in price action trading?
- Answer: To maximize profits and minimize risks, traders should follow a strict risk management strategy, use stop-loss orders and clear profit targets, diversify their portfolio, and stay informed about the latest news and economic events that could influence the markets.

How can traders use oscillators to identify overbought or oversold conditions in the market?
- Answer: Oscillators, such as the Relative Strength Index (RSI) or Stochastic, can help traders identify overbought or oversold conditions in the market. When these indicators reach extreme levels, it may indicate that the market is overbought or oversold, which could potentially lead to trend reversals.

What are the best strategies for trading trend reversals with price action trading?
- Answer: To trade trend reversals, traders can use techniques such as identifying candlestick patterns, confirming signals using additional technical indicators, and looking for divergences between price movements and momentum indicators.

How can traders evaluate and improve their performance in price action trading?
- Answer: Traders can evaluate their performance by keeping a trading journal, regularly analyzing their trades to identify strengths and weaknesses, and making adjustments to their strategy accordingly. They can also benefit from feedback from peers, mentors, or coaches to gain external perspectives on their trading decisions.

What are the key factors to consider when identifying support and resistance levels on price charts?
- Response: Key factors include the recurrence of rebounds or consolidations at these levels, the clarity of the support or resistance zone, as well as confirmation by other indicators or technical analysis tools.

How can traders use moving averages to filter trading signals and confirm trends in financial markets?
- Response: Moving averages can be used to smooth price data and identify the general direction of a trend. Crosses between different periods of moving averages can signal potential trend changes or entry and exit points.

What are the best practices to avoid false signals and common pitfalls when using price action trading?
- Response: Some best practices include validating signals with multiple indicators or tools, confirming trends through thorough analysis, as well as patience and discipline to avoid impulsive reactions to price movements.

What is the impact of economic news and global events on price action trading strategies?
- Response: Economic news and global events can significantly impact financial markets and influence price movements. Traders must be aware of these factors and be prepared to adjust their strategies accordingly to avoid potential losses.

How can traders effectively manage periods of increased volatility in markets when utilizing price action trading?

- Response: Risk management is essential during periods of increased volatility. Traders can reduce their position sizes, raise their stop-loss levels, and remain cautious while waiting for volatility to calm down before making significant trading decisions.

What are the key characteristics to look for when identifying emerging trends on price charts?
- Response: Some key characteristics include series of higher highs and higher lows, ascending or descending trendlines, as well as increasing or decreasing trading volumes, depending on the direction of the trend.

How can traders differentiate strong trading signals from weak signals when using price action trading?
- Response: Strong signals are often confirmed by multiple factors, such as the convergence of several technical indicators, a strong price reaction at a support or resistance level, or a clearly established trend confirmed by high volume.

What are the best strategies for managing open trades and maximizing potential profits while minimizing losses?
- Response: Some effective strategies include moving stop-loss levels to lock in profits, scaling out positions to take partial profits, as well as regularly monitoring trades for signs of trend reversal or consolidation.

What is the impact of trading psychology on the decisions of traders using price action trading?
- Response: Trading psychology can play a major role in traders' decisions, sometimes leading them to make impulsive or emotional decisions. Traders must develop discipline and emotional control to avoid costly mistakes and stay focused on their trading strategy.

How can traders leverage specific candlestick patterns to identify trading opportunities in financial markets?
- Response: Traders can use candlestick patterns such as the doji, hammer, or morning star to spot potential turning points in price trends, identify support and resistance levels, and confirm price action-based trading signals.

What are the key factors to consider when identifying support and resistance levels on price charts?

- Response: Key factors include the recurrence of rebounds or consolidations at these levels, the clarity of the support or resistance zone, as well as confirmation by other indicators or technical analysis tools.

How can traders use moving averages to filter trading signals and confirm trends in financial markets?
- Response: Moving averages can be used to smooth price data and identify the general direction of a trend. Crosses between different periods of moving averages can signal potential trend changes or entry and exit points.

What are the best practices to avoid false signals and common pitfalls when using price action trading?
- Response: Some best practices include validating signals with multiple indicators or tools, confirming trends through thorough analysis, as well as patience and discipline to avoid impulsive reactions to price movements.

What is the impact of economic news and global events on price action trading strategies?
- Response: Economic news and global events can significantly impact financial markets and influence price movements. Traders must be aware of these factors and be prepared to adjust their strategies accordingly to avoid potential losses.

How can traders effectively manage periods of increased volatility in markets when utilizing price action trading?
- Response: Risk management is essential during periods of increased volatility. Traders can reduce their position sizes, raise their stop-loss levels, and remain cautious while waiting for volatility to calm down before making significant trading decisions.

What are the key characteristics to look for when identifying emerging trends on price charts?
- Response: Some key characteristics include series of higher highs and higher lows, ascending or descending trendlines, as well as increasing or decreasing trading volumes, depending on the direction of the trend.

How can traders differentiate strong trading signals from weak signals when using price action trading?

- Response: Strong signals are often confirmed by multiple factors, such as the convergence of several technical indicators, a strong price reaction at a support or resistance level, or a clearly established trend confirmed by high volume.

What are the best strategies for managing open trades and maximizing potential profits while minimizing losses?
- Response: Some effective strategies include moving stop-loss levels to lock in profits, scaling out positions to take partial profits, as well as regularly monitoring trades for signs of trend reversal or consolidation.

What is the impact of trading psychology on the decisions of traders using price action trading?
- Response: Trading psychology can play a major role in traders' decisions, sometimes leading them to make impulsive or emotional decisions. Traders must develop discipline and emotional control to avoid costly mistakes and stay focused on their trading strategy.

How can traders leverage specific candlestick patterns to identify trading opportunities in financial markets?
- Response: Traders can use candlestick patterns such as the doji, hammer, or morning star to spot potential turning points in price trends, identify support and resistance levels, and confirm price action-based trading signals.

Personal Notes:

Websites, resources, ideas, etc...

www.ingramcontent.com/pod-product-compliance
Lightning Source LLC
Chambersburg PA
CBHW050324230526
45471CB00005B/2346